AMERICA
IN THE
20TH
CENTURY

1970-1979

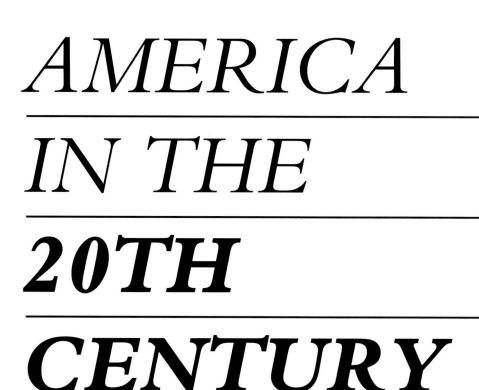

AMERICA
IN THE
20TH
CENTURY

SECOND EDITION
Revised and Expanded with Primary Sources

1970-1979

Janet McDonnell

MARSHALL CAVENDISH
NEW YORK • LONDON • TORONTO • SYDNEY

Marshall Cavendish
99 White Plains Road
Tarrytown, NY 10591

Website: www.marshallcavendish.com

Library of Congress Cataloging-in-Publication Data

America in the 20th Century.-- 2nd ed., rev. and expanded with primary sources.
    p. cm.
    Includes bibliographical references and index.
    ISBN 0-7614-7364-5 (set)
    1. United States -- Civilization -- 20th century. I. Title: America in the twentieth century.
    E169.1.A471872   2003
    973.9--dc21

                                              2001052949
    ISBN 0-7614-7372-6 (vol. 8)

Printed in Malaysia
Bound in the United States of America

06 05 04 03 02 5 4 3 2 1

Series created by Discovery Books

Series Editor: Paul Humphrey
Academic Consultants: Gregory Bush,
Chair of History Department, University of Miami, Coral Gables
Richard J. Taylor, History Department, University of Wisconsin, Parkside
Marshall Cavendish Editor: Peter Mavrikis
Marshall Cavendish Production Manager: Alan Tsai
Project Editors: Valerie Weber and Helen Dwyer
Picture Research: Gillian Humphrey
Design Concept: Laurie Shock
Designers: Ian Winton and Winsome Malcolm

*(Frontispiece) A feminist group displays its emblem and
banners in front of the Statue of Liberty.*

Contents

CHAPTER 1
In the Wake of the Sixties — What Now?

In the 1960s, many students became politically active, unified by their opposition to the Vietnam War and eager to create a fair society. As dissent became more violent, a conservative backlash arose. In 1968, Richard Nixon was elected president, partly because he promised to restore law and order.

In comparison with other decades, the seventies present a hazier, more confusing image than most. In fact, some people think of the seventies as the hangover suffered after the turbulent sixties. Now *there's* a decade that evokes some powerful memories. Just a few words conjure up the explosive mixture of idealism and tragedy, of hope and violence, that characterize the sixties — Martin Luther King, Jr., Vietnam, Woodstock, the Summer of Love.

The seventies, on the other hand, get no respect. When the seventies are mentioned, people tend to remember bell-bottom jeans, polyester leisure suits, the Bee Gees, and the Brady Bunch. But once one looks beyond such questionable contributions to pop culture, the seventies are revealed as a dynamic period in U.S. history. For during those ten years, the nation underwent some profound changes.

Some of the changes were extensions of trends begun in the tumultuous sixties. At the same time, a reactionary conservative movement began gathering force in the seventies. Also, in the course of the decade, some unexpected and unprecedented world events would have a direct impact on the lives of all American citizens and on the status of their country.

By the end of the sixties, the American public was tired of the turmoil and social unrest that had racked their country for most of the decade. They longed for a return to a more peaceful atmosphere, but in fact, the upheaval would spill over into the seventies.

Of course, the forces that led to the turmoil had been building for years: racism, poverty, pollution, the Cold War, to name a few. These were all complicated problems with deep roots, and it is therefore no surprise that the stormy atmosphere of the sixties would take a long time to settle. The way people responded to those problems also created deep divisions in American society and led to painful conflicts that would leave lasting scars.

Conflict Between Young and Old

An important source of dissension in the sixties was the so-called generation gap. During that decade, the baby boomer generation came of age. Emboldened by their numbers, these young people were swept up in the belief that they could change the world. College students and young political activists were filled with a vision of a more just and open society, a "new consciousness." But like the presidency of John F. Kennedy, which began with the promise of "Camelot" and ended in tragedy, the idealism of the youth movement was increasingly overshadowed by anger and violence. Student protesters grew impatient with traditional institutions and attitudes that stood in the way of their vision. Many proclaimed their allegiance to the New Left, a move-ment dedicated to resisting the "Establishment" (the dominant institutions and individuals who supported the status quo), which they believed was corrupt, immoral, and obsolete. One of the strongest unifying causes of the New Left and of the youth movement in general was opposition to the Vietnam War. They believed it was an unjust war that pitted American imperialism against a poor Third World country's right to self-determination.

As the sixties wore on, some members of the New Left began employing more and more inflammatory measures, which sometimes led to violence. In part, this development was a reaction to the escalation of America's involvement in the Vietnam War. But the media also played a role. By making celebrities of the most outrageous leaders of the youth movement, and by considering flag-burning more newsworthy than a quiet protest, the media, in a sense,

> *"Although sixties radicals [cultural and political] spent the early seventies loudly bemoaning the end of the revolution, what was in fact going on was the working of the phenomena of the sixties into the mainstream of American life."*
>
> Nicholas Lemann, *American Heritage* magazine

By 1970, there was no sign of U.S. troops winning the conflict in Vietnam. War veterans, such as these in Miami, protested about atrocities they had seen, or in which they had taken part. Some of the GIs who objected to the war started their own antiwar move-ments — including Vietnam Veterans Against the War — producing underground newspapers at military bases. Many desert-ers fled to Western Europe and Canada. In Vietnam itself, troops steadily became more and more demoralized.

> "We have to force the disintegration of society, creating strategic armed chaos where there is now order."
>
> The aims of the Weather Underground, a radical paramilitary group

encouraged those methods. As writer Todd Gitlin explains, "Where a picket line might have been news in 1965, it took tear gas and bloodied heads to make headlines in 1968."

In the late sixties, a paramilitary group of young radicals calling itself the Weather Underground was formed. In 1970, the group began a series of bombings, usually directed against government or police facilities. Such extremist acts and the media's highlighting of them frightened and outraged Americans, many of whom did not understand the difference between peaceful student protesters and those who employed guerilla tactics.

The activities of radical protesters, many of whom were college students or former students, most antagonized members of the working class. This was partly because the children of the blue-collar workers were the most vulnerable to the draft, while those able to afford college could find ways around serving in Vietnam. As one worker said, "We can't understand how all those rich kids — the kids with beads from the fancy suburbs — how they get off when my son has to go over there and maybe get his head shot off."

Many in the white working class were also irritated by demands made by minorities on the government. They resented the expansion of the welfare rolls through Great Society programs, for though unemployment was high in the construction trades and many workers were struggling to get by, they didn't see the government coming to *their* aid.

In May of 1970, thousands of construction workers in New York City demonstrated their frustration by organizing "hard hat rallies." Wearing their construction helmets and waving American flags, the workers marched almost daily throughout the month, proclaiming their support of Nixon's policy in Vietnam. Some of the marchers turned violent, assaulting student protesters or anyone else who looked like a "longhair." A group of workers stormed City Hall and demanded that the flag be raised to full-staff. The flag had been flying at half-staff as a symbol of mourning for four student protesters who had been killed by National Guardsmen at Kent State University in Ohio.

The hard hat riots were but one symbol of how deeply divided was American society as the sixties turned into the seventies. Though the youth movement and the New Left had influenced the direction of the country for most of the sixties, a conservative backlash had begun pushing in the opposite direction. In 1968, Richard Nixon was elected president on a law-and-order platform. Working- and middle-class Americans were fed up with the demands, the protests, and the chaos. To many, the Movement, Revolution, Rebellion, or whatever it was called, was an affront to all that they held dear: loyalty to family, patriotism, and belief in the American dream. That dream had backfired for many families who, after working hard and saving enough money to send their sons and daughters to college, were shocked to find that not only were their offspring not grateful for the opportunity, but they also returned home from school denouncing their parents' lifestyles and values. As the most radical elements of the youth movement became more violent in their threats to the traditions and institutions of American society, Nixon's promise to "balance freedom with order" was well-received by mainstream America.

Newly nominated Richard Nixon and his vice-presidential candidate Spiro Agnew wave to delegates at the 1968 convention. They were helped in their campaign by Democratic indecision over their choice of candidates. However, many blue-collar southern Democrats voted for George Wallace, the independent candidate, and the election was very close.

Race Relations at a Crossroads

Another source of turmoil in the sixties was the civil rights movement. The venerated civil rights leader Martin Luther King, Jr., led a campaign of civil disobedience that forced the American public to focus on the gross inequalities that existed in their society. In horror, Americans watched the television coverage of peaceful protesters being attacked by police dogs, water cannons, and batons. The civil rights movement met with hostile resistance from white segregationists in the South, who resented any attempts to change their racist ways. Many moderate politicians agreed with the need to address civil rights but feared that King and his followers were demanding too much change too quickly.

To that argument, King replied:

We have waited for more than 340 years for our constitutional and God-given rights. . . . There comes a time when the cup of endurance runs over, and men are no longer willing to be plunged into an abyss of injustice where they experience the blackness of corroding despair.

The civil rights movement made great strides in the sixties, creating substantial changes in laws and attitudes. In 1964, President Johnson signed the Civil Rights Act, sweeping legislation that outlawed segregation in all public facilities and set up organizations aimed at providing job opportunities for African-Americans.

Despite the exhilarating victories of the civil rights movement, African-Americans living in the ghettos of large cities were still faced with the crippling problems of poverty, slum

CIVIL RIGHTS

For further information see primary source entries on pages

11: 1582-83; **12:** 1627-32, 1635-38, 1643-50, 1652-55

housing, and unemployment. In the mid-1960s, race riots flared up in cities throughout the nation. The violence reached horrifying levels after the assassination of King, as riots broke out in 125 cities across twenty-nine states.

Stokely Carmichael was an opponent of nonviolent civil rights protest. He vowed, "If we don't get justice, we're going to tear this country apart." The Black Power movement fostered the idea that "Black is Beautiful" and eventually led to a more widespread awareness of African-American history and contributions to the nation.

But even before King's death, many African-Americans were feeling a growing frustration at the slow pace of progress and a smoldering resentment of their position in society. Impatient and angry, an increasing number of African-Americans were rejecting the nonviolent, integrationist philosophy of the traditional civil rights movement and were instead embracing the Black Power movement, which called for a black revolution by means of "aggressive armed violence" if necessary. The Black Muslim movement also won many converts by preaching black separatism, a message that appealed to those who believed integration would

weaken black culture and ultimately fail to create racial equality.

Some feared that the Black Power and Black Muslim movements threatened to undo the progress that had been made. The militant, inflammatory rhetoric of black leaders resulted in a white backlash. Conservatives demanded that the government crack down on black revolutionaries, and Richard Nixon won wide support by campaigning against open housing and busing to achieve school desegregation.

As the new decade began, race relations appeared to be at a crossroads in the United States. Some people believed that the hopes of the civil rights movement died with Martin Luther King. But other black activists were pursuing a new path to equal rights — politics. The Voting Rights Act of 1965 instituted a five-year ban (which was then extended in 1970) on all literacy tests and other measures used to keep blacks from voting. As a result, millions of African-Americans were soon registered to vote, and in the following years, many civil rights leaders were elected to government office.

The Changing Role of Women

The demands for equal rights and the student rebellions of the late sixties inspired another movement that would become a powerful influence in the seventies — the women's movement. In 1960, women were still treated as second-class citizens in many ways in the United States, and reports showed that a disproportionate number of women were living in poverty. In addition, many women were deeply frustrated by a society that defined their roles narrowly as wives and mothers. Betty Friedan tapped into those frustrations in her book, *The Feminine Mystique.* Encouraged by Friedan's book and by the civil rights movement, feminists began organizing for equal rights. The National Organization for Women (NOW) was formed in 1966 "to confront with concrete action, the conditions which now prevent women from enjoying the equality of opportunity and freedom of choice which is their right as individual Americans, and as human beings."

Initially some men were threatened by the women's movement, and many women were afraid of challenging the established order. "Women's libbers" were often ridiculed and portrayed as man-haters or radical lesbians. But the leaders of the women's movement were not dissuaded. At the dawn of the seventies, feminists were making headlines by borrowing tactics from student protesters and civil rights activists to get their message across. In 1970, on the fiftieth anniversary of the amendment that gave women the right to vote, fifty thousand people marched down Fifth Avenue in New York City. That same year, one hundred women held a sit-in at the offices of *Ladies Home Journal* to protest the narrow image of women portrayed by the magazine. But this was only the beginning. During the seventies, the role of women in American society would undergo some serious changes.

Middle-class Resentment

Though race relations and the women's movement were important social issues confronting the U.S. in 1970, the economy was on the minds of many middle-class Americans. As the decade began, inflation was on the rise, taxes were taking a bigger bite of people's income, and interest rates were climbing. Some people blamed the weakening economy on Lyndon Johnson's Great Society programs, which were instituted as part of his "war on poverty." By the end of the sixties, critics were calling the programs inefficient and too expensive. Many working- and middle-class Americans saw the programs as nothing more than government handouts that discouraged independence. As one fed-up taxpayer put it, "If I had anything to say about it, all these people wouldn't be on give-away programs. The government is trying to tax middle-class people down to the welfare level."

Opposition to the Vietnam War

But concern over the economy and welfare reform paled in comparison to a more immediate and explosive dilemma facing the nation as it entered the seventies — the Vietnam War. In 1970, the country was still heavily involved in Vietnam, and the antiwar movement had built to a fevered pitch. American commitments to Vietnam can be traced all the way back to 1950, when the battle lines of the Cold War were being drawn. President Harry Truman, in accordance with the policy of containment, pledged to help defend South Vietnam against the Communist North Vietnamese and Communist insurgents in South Vietnam. At first, support came in the

"This is not a bedroom war. This is a political movement."

Betty Friedan

VIETNAM WAR

For further information
see primary source entries
on pages

12: 1638-43, 1660-63

form of advisors and monetary aid. By the mid-1960s, however, it had become apparent that more direct involvement would be necessary to keep South Vietnam secure. When President Johnson sent the first U.S. combat troops to Vietnam in 1965, promising that their presence would be temporary, there was very little public dissent at home.

In the following years, however, as more and more American soldiers were killed without any clear signs of progress, a growing number of angry Americans took to the streets in strident antiwar protests. President Johnson's inability to clearly define America's objectives in the war only aggravated the situation. Hounded by antiwar demonstrators, Johnson decided that he would not seek reelection in 1968.

By 1970, a majority of Americans wanted the United States out of the war in one way or another. A sense of resignation had settled in, especially

In what became one of the most publicized images of the war, Vietnamese children are shown caught in a napalm attack in 1972. Atrocities against civilians turned many Americans against the war.

President Nixon visits the troops in Vietnam in 1969. Although he knew American victory was impossible, Nixon tried to reinforce the South Vietnamese while pulling U.S. troops out of the country — a policy called Vietnamization. By 1972, it was obvious that South Vietnam alone could not hold out against the Communists, and all hope of an honorable withdrawal had vanished.

after the 1968 North Vietnamese Tet Offensive. The magnitude and scope of the Communist offensive, a massive attack against South Vietnamese military and civilian targets, had shocked both the American troops in Vietnam and Americans at home watching the news on television. Two things became painfully clear: The United States had greatly underestimated its enemy, and the Communists were willing to accept enormous casualties in pursuit of what they considered a sacred goal — a Vietnam unified under communism. The Communists were also motivated by nationalism, for they saw the United States troops as foreign invaders. Most Americans, on the other hand, were not willing to sacrifice any more of their sons, husbands, or brothers to a brutal war in a distant country for an uncertain cause. Over 33,500 had died already.

President Nixon, realizing that opposition to the war and restraints on the U.S. military made an outright victory impossible, promised to gradually withdraw American combat troops. But Nixon also believed that it was crucial that the U.S. not be seen as abandoning its ally — even if that ally was, in reality, its own puppet government. His goal was "peace with honor." A politician known as a tough anticommunist, Nixon was determined to prove to the North Vietnamese that the U.S. would not be pushed into accepting peace at any cost, despite the protests at home. In March of 1969, only two months after taking office, Nixon approved a plan to begin bombing Communist sanctuaries in Cambodia, South Vietnam's neighbor to the west. The bombing continued in secret for fourteen months, since North Vietnam could not publicly protest without admitting that it had illegally and stealthily advanced on Cambodian territory. However, a penchant for such clandestine acts would become a trademark of the Nixon presidency and ultimately lead to his humiliating fall from power.

Meanwhile, the protests at home grew louder and larger. In 1969, Americans were horrified by revelations of the My Lai massacre, in which U.S. soldiers murdered hundreds of innocent Vietnamese civilians. For many, the atrocity confirmed the warning of Massachusetts Governor Francis Sargent when he said, "This war is costing America its soul." Nixon, promising that peace was within sight, called for unity and support, while his vice president, Spiro Agnew, attacked the antiwar demonstrators as traitors. By 1970, approximately 60,000 of the over 540,000 American troops had returned home and peace negotiations were underway in Paris, but as the decade began, Americans were still dying in Vietnam. Peace remained elusive.

Entangled in an unpopular war, staggered by years of social upheaval, and facing an uncertain future, the seventies were off to a shaky start. For those Americans hoping for a return to stability, the seventies would not exactly bring satisfaction. The burning passions of the sixties would gradually cool, but the seventies would provide plenty of new sparks.

A wounded American soldier is taken for medical treatment during a battle in Vietnam. More than fifty-seven thousand Americans died in the war. Battered by their experiences in Vietnam, those who came home were more likely to succumb to alcoholism, drug addiction, divorce, depression, and suicide than those who had not served in the war.

CHAPTER 2
Striving for
"Peace with Honor"

The Future at Stake

When Richard Nixon took over as commander in chief of the armed forces, he knew that it would be his task to extricate United States combat troops from the war in Vietnam. But he was determined, as was his predecessor, to not be the first U.S. president in history to lose a war.

Of course, Nixon was not only concerned about his own reputation. Both he and Henry Kissinger, his national security advisor and the main architect of his foreign policy, were well aware that the reputation of the United States was on the line. Ever since the Cold War began, the U.S. had been committed to defending the independence of free states all over the world against the hostile threat of communism. Critics of this policy argued that it was too ambitious and that it sometimes made allies of despots simply because they were not Communists. Still, many others believed that the security of the free world rested upon America's ability to fight the spread of communism wherever it occurred. If the U.S. were to simply withdraw from Vietnam entirely, as the most fervent antiwar activists wanted, it would be admitting defeat, thereby jeopardizing its role as defender of the free world. Without the U.S. occupying that position, the fear was that other, weaker countries would be at risk. As a long-time enemy of communism, Nixon was resolute that this would not happen.

In an effort to disengage U.S. troops from the war without leaving South Vietnam vulnerable to the Communists, the Nixon administration devised a policy that came to be known as "Vietnamization." The plan was to enable South Vietnam to take more responsibility for its own defense by providing their military (the Army of the Republic of Vietnam, or ARVN) with training, advisors, and equipment. In other words, the U.S. would return to the role it had in Vietnam before 1965 — as an advisor and supporter.

While the U.S. rushed to reinforce the South Vietnamese army, peace negotiations were at a standstill in Paris. The North Vietnamese rejected a proposed mutual withdrawal of all U.S. and North Vietnamese troops from South Vietnam, and the U.S. refused to consider the resignation of South Vietnam's President Nguyen Van Thieu as a condition for peace.

With U.S. troops pulling out of Vietnam, Nixon worried that the Communists would see no reason to give ground at the peace negotiations. To prove to them that the U.S. was not abandoning its defense of South Vietnam, Nixon believed a show of military might was necessary.

> *"America has never been defeated in the proud, 199-year history of this country and we shall not be defeated in Vietnam."*
>
> Richard Nixon, 1970

The War Widens

In March of 1970, the leader of Cambodia, Prince Norodom Sihanouk, was overthrown while traveling in Europe. Anarchy ensued in Cambodia. Secretary of State William Rogers assured the American public that the developments in Cambodia "will not cause the war to be widened in any way." But Nixon had other ideas.

A Cambodian woman among the ruins of Phnom Penh. President Nixon sent troops to invade Cambodia in 1970 to destroy Communist bases there. Many Americans protested this incursion into a neutral country, and the antiwar movement grew. In 1975, the city was taken by the Communist Khmer Rouge, who attempted to eradicate all opposition.

The president realized that sending ground troops into Cambodia would cause domestic uproar, for the antiwar movement was growing larger and louder than ever. Despite that knowledge, Nixon decided that drastic action was necessary for several reasons. As the chaos and blood-bath continued in Cambodia, the Communist movement there, called the Khmer Rouge, was gaining ground, and North Vietnamese troops were pushing further into the country. Also, with American troops withdrawing from Vietnam, Nixon felt the need to obliterate the enemy bases in Cambodia once and for all to protect not only South Vietnam but also the remaining U.S. troops, who were becoming increasingly vulnerable as their numbers dwindled. Though the U.S. had secretly been bombing the Communist sanctuaries from the air for over a year, ground troops now seemed necessary. Finally, Nixon still hoped that a strong show of force could convince the North Vietnamese to move towards a compromise in the peace talks.

In a speech to the American public on April 30, 1970, announcing the Cambodian incursion, Nixon hoped to rally the country's support and undercut his critics by outlining America's purpose in dramatic terms:

If, when the chips are down, the world's most powerful nation, the United States of America, acts like a pitiful help-less giant, the forces of totalitarianism and anarchy will threaten free nations and free institutions throughout the world.

Plenty of Americans were not convinced. To them, Nixon was breaking his campaign promise to "win the peace and end the war" by

In May 1970, students at Kent State University in Ohio protested U.S. involvement in Cambodia, firebombing the Reserve Officers' Training Corps building. The Ohio governor called in the National Guard. Four students were shot dead. This event led to demonstrations at hundreds of universities, most of which had to be closed down. A hundred thousand students went to Washington to protest the killings.

spreading the conflict into a neutral country. College campuses across the nation erupted in fervent protest at the news. At Kent State University in Ohio, the antiwar demonstrations took a tragic turn. When student demonstrators attacked the Reserve Officers' Training Corps building on campus, anxious National Guardsmen fired into the crowd, killing four. That tragedy set off further protests, including a march of almost a hundred thousand on Washington, where demonstrators surrounded the White House and other government buildings. By this time, even some Vietnam veterans had joined the antiwar movement.

Rather than try to soothe the growing fears of the public and Congress over the direction the war was taking, Nixon grew defiant in his pursuit of peace with honor. But the enormous antagonism also made him nervous. Soon after the march on Washington, Nixon called on an army intelligence specialist to coordinate surveillance of his domestic critics.

The *Pentagon Papers*

Feelings of distrust and suspicion by the public of the president intensified when the first excerpts of the *Pentagon Papers* were published in the *New York Times* and other newspapers in June of 1971. Commissioned by Robert McNamara, former secretary of defense in the Johnson administration, the *Pentagon Papers* were a collection of confidential memos and analyses regarding U.S. policy and actions in Vietnam. Their publication further inflamed the antiwar movement by revealing that President Johnson had deceived the American public. The U.S. had been involved in Southeast Asia earlier and to a greater extent than the Johnson administration had led the public to believe.

Daniel Ellsberg, a former Defense Department aide who had grown adamantly opposed to the war, was indicted for stealing government property and violating the Espionage

Act by leaking these classified documents to the press. But for Nixon, that was not enough. Though the *Pentagon Papers* did not contain information damaging to the current administration, Nixon was shocked and outraged that the press felt it had the authority to decide what was and was not confidential information. Nixon tried to prevent further damage by seeking injunctions against the newspapers involved, but the Supreme Court rejected the appeal.

The Pentagon Papers *were published in paperback. This collection of Defense Department documents about the war in Vietnam was leaked by Daniel Ellsberg. The antiwar movement was strengthened by revelations of greater American involvement in Southeast Asia than had previously been made public.*

Still, the incident made Nixon more determined than ever to squelch the dissent and plug the press leaks that were undermining his strategy in Vietnam. Nixon's aide Charles Colson drew up a list of perceived "enemies" that included politicians, journalists, academics, entertainers, and others, many of whom would be subjected to wiretaps and other forms of surveillance. A clandestine unit referred to as the "plumbers" was also formed. Their original mission was to plug the press leaks, but the plumbers were an ambitious group. In an attempt to find information that would discredit Ellsberg or reveal his future strategy, several of the plumbers broke into the office of Ellsberg's psychiatrist. Seven months later, five men linked to the plumbers were arrested for burglary in the Watergate complex.

The Decline of Morale

By the summer of 1971, 58 percent of Americans polled said they felt that America was involved in an immoral war. This growing antipathy toward the war was not confined to civilians, however. The morale of the troops in Vietnam was quickly eroding. The war that American soldiers were expected to fight in Vietnam was like no other that the United States had ever been involved in. It was an undeclared war with no front lines, in which even women and children could be terrorist agents of the Communist insurgents, known as the Viet Cong, in South Vietnam. Danger was everywhere.

As the first troops were withdrawn, it became clear that the goal of ultimate victory had been abandoned. Now the troops who remained were fighting to give the United States a better bargaining position at the peace negotiations. For many soldiers, that was not a mission worth losing one's life over, and for them, the mission became their own survival.

News of the growing antiwar movement back home made its way to the troops, and some showed their approval by wearing peace signs on their helmets and uniforms. Other soldiers, desperate to return home alive, took much more drastic, violent measures. In 1970, there were two hundred reported incidents of "fragging," wherein soldiers killed their own leaders with fragmentation grenades, often to avoid being led into dangerous situations. As one soldier explained, "Grenades leave no fingerprints."

Other evidence of the growing demoralization was the spread of drug abuse through the troops. In Vietnam, marijuana, heroin, opium, and other drugs were cheap and readily available. As the ugly war dragged on, more and more GIs were turning to drugs to escape the boredom, the tension, and the horrors of what they had done and seen. In 1970, the U.S. command in Saigon estimated that sixty-five thousand soldiers were using drugs. The widespread problem gave GIs one more danger to worry about — the possibility that their fellow soldier was so high on drugs that he would put others' lives at risk.

The Easter Offensive

The Cambodian invasion that had stirred such dissent in the U.S. did not achieve what Nixon had hoped.

The North Vietnamese were still unyielding in negotiations, and their military capabilities had not been greatly diminished. In fact, by the spring of 1972, they were prepared

to launch a major offensive. The Communists had several aims that they hoped to achieve through a large-scale assault, not the least of which was to influence the presidential election campaign that was beginning in the United States. But their primary objective was to inflict such a blow on the South Vietnamese forces that the U.S. would realize that the policy of Vietnamization was a failure

The South Vietnamese Army prepares to meet the Communist offensive in April 1972. American bombers had to intervene to push the Communists back. This attack proved to North Vietnam and to the U.S. that South Vietnam could not defend itself without American help.

and that the only way to end the war was to agree to the North Vietnamese conditions for peace.

On March 30, the so-called Easter offensive began. Over 120,000 Communist soldiers attacked in three waves. Though U.S. intelligence had anticipated a Communist attack, the magnitude and duration of the offensive came as a surprise. In several cases, inexperienced and poorly led South Vietnamese troops fled in terror, and at least one regional commander's performance was described by an American advisor as "disgraceful." Part of the problem was that many of the South's generals had attained their positions not through prowess on the battlefields but through loyalty to President Thieu. Almost all of the U.S. ground troops by now had been withdrawn, but a massive show of American air power was called on to repulse the attacks. B-52 bombers pounded the advancing Communist troops and their bases. In addition, Nixon ordered massive air attacks on targets in North Vietnam. In May, Nixon ordered the mining of Haiphong harbor and set up a naval blockade to cut off supplies to the North Vietnamese troops.

In the end, the Communists lost an estimated fifty thousand soldiers and were forced to retreat from the areas they had captured. Even so, the Easter offensive could not be characterized as a complete failure for North Vietnam; it had achieved at least one of its goals. Though some South Vietnamese troops were exceptionally brave in battle, the undeniable truth was that, without U.S. air power and advisors supporting them, the South's troops would not have been able to hold their territory. Though Nixon publicly praised the South Vietnamese performance, privately he knew that Vietnamization was not working. The Communist drive and the South's performance had also unnerved the government in Saigon, which was growing more and more worried about its ability to defend itself without the United States.

A Breakthrough in Negotiations

Though there had been no movement at the official peace negotiations in Paris, Henry Kissinger had been secretly meeting with the chief North Vietnamese negotiator, Le Duc Tho, on and off since early 1970. The talks had often been heated and exhausting, but by the fall of 1972, both sides seemed weary of the war and ready for compromise. On October 8, just weeks before the presidential election, they reached a provisional agreement.

The North Vietnamese backed down on their insistence that Thieu be removed from power. Instead, a "council of national reconciliation," which was to include representatives from Thieu's government, the Communist Viet Cong, and neutral countries, would supervise elections in Saigon. It was hoped this would lead to a lasting peace. After a cease-fire, the U.S. was to complete the withdrawal of its troops and a prisoner exchange would take place. The United States, in an important concession, no longer demanded the withdrawal of all North Vietnamese troops from South Vietnam. Instead, the Communists could continue to hold whatever territory they controlled at the time of the cease-fire until elections could decide the political fate of South Vietnam.

> "The real problem is that the enemy is willing to sacrifice in order to win, while the South Vietnamese simply aren't willing to pay that much of a price in order to avoid losing."
>
> Entry in Richard Nixon's diary

At last, it seemed the United States was close to extracting itself from the quagmire in Vietnam, but one important obstacle stood in the way — President Thieu. The South Vietnamese leader was understandably opposed to the "leopard spot" arrangement, in which Communist-controlled areas would be allowed to remain in South Vietnam, and he was outraged that the United States agreed to leave his government in such a precarious position. Nixon needed Thieu's approval or America would be seen as abandoning South Vietnam. But when the U.S. tried to amend the agreement to Thieu's liking, the North Vietnamese dug in their heels, and talks broke off again in December.

Frustrated by the stalemate and eager to get out of the war once and for all, Nixon took a two-pronged approach. After ordering $1 billion in military equipment to be sent to South Vietnam, he threatened to cut off further aid unless Thieu softened his resistance. As for the North Vietnamese, Nixon ordered massive air strikes on targets in and around Hanoi, the capital of North Vietnam, beginning on December 18, 1972.

The thousands of bombs caused heavy damage, destroying factories, railroads, power plants, and other important facilities. The so-called Christmas bombing was highly controversial, for critics were outraged that the U.S. would take such aggressive action when peace was supposedly just around the corner. In fact, shortly before the November election, Kissinger had announced, "We believe peace is at hand." In the light of the Christmas bombing, many Americans now believed that Kissinger's statement had been nothing more than a ploy to ensure Nixon's reelection. But even more painful was the fact that ninety-three

Henry Kissinger and Le Duc Tho, the North Vietnamese peace negotiator, come to an agreement in January 1973. Later that year, Congress decided that the U.S. would never again become involved in military action in Southeast Asia.

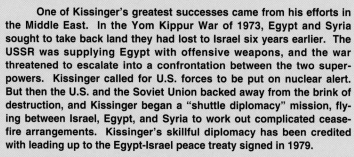

Henry Kissinger.

Henry Kissinger arrived in the United States as a teenager after his Jewish family fled Nazi Germany. By 1973, he was perceived by many to be the second most powerful man in his adopted country.

When Richard Nixon appointed Kissinger as the head of the National Security Council in 1969, the two men agreed on a strategy for streamlining foreign policy decision making, a strategy that gave Kissinger a great deal of power. Both Kissinger and Nixon believed the bureaucracy of the Defense and State Departments was an obstacle to effective foreign policy, and they both believed that a great deal more could be accomplished through secret channels of diplomacy.

Liberals considered Kissinger as responsible as Nixon for U.S. policy in Vietnam and were therefore sharply critical of him. But, in general, Kissinger was popular with the American public. Unlike Nixon, Kissinger courted the press, and the press, in turn, was intrigued by Kissinger's intellectual reputation and his secret diplomatic missions. Though he could be arrogant, Kissinger was able to disarm his critics by poking fun at himself in his thick German accent. He also achieved the reputation of a ladies' man, often appearing in public accompanied by glamorous women. When asked his secret, Kissinger responded, "Power is the great aphrodisiac."

One of Kissinger's greatest successes came from his efforts in the Middle East. In the Yom Kippur War of 1973, Egypt and Syria sought to take back land they had lost to Israel six years earlier. The USSR was supplying Egypt with offensive weapons, and the war threatened to escalate into a confrontation between the two superpowers. Kissinger called for U.S. forces to be put on nuclear alert. But then the U.S. and the Soviet Union backed away from the brink of destruction, and Kissinger began a "shuttle diplomacy" mission, flying between Israel, Egypt, and Syria to work out complicated cease-fire arrangements. Kissinger's skillful diplomacy has been credited with leading up to the Egypt-Israel peace treaty signed in 1979.

Despite his successes, Kissinger's reputation was hurt by the Watergate scandal when it was revealed that he approved the wiretapping of several journalists and government officials. Though Kissinger claimed the action was necessary to stop news leaks and to protect national security, his image was permanently tainted. His popularity also fell after revelations that he was involved in the CIA plot to overthrow the democratically elected Marxist government of Salvador Allende in Chile.

Though President Ford kept Kissinger on as secretary of state (a position to which Nixon appointed him in 1973), by the mid-seventies he had many critics. Conservatives accused Kissinger of giving too much to the Communists in negotiations, and liberals criticized him for being too secretive and unconcerned with human rights. Despite this, Kissinger is still credited with moving U.S. foreign policy beyond the Cold War.

American pilots and crew members were lost during the mission, thirty-one of them taken prisoner.

Finally, after eleven days of bombing, the North Vietnamese agreed to reopen peace talks if the air strikes were halted. On January 27, 1973, a peace agreement almost identical to the one arranged in October was formally signed. President Thieu accepted the agreement under pressure from Nixon, with his written pledge to intervene should the Communists break the cease-fire, though Thieu was still deeply dissatisfied with its terms.

A Doubtful Peace

Though Nixon declared that the U.S. had achieved its goal of peace with honor, most observers believed it was just a matter of time before the cease-fire was broken and the Communists overran South Vietnam. Still the Nixon administration sought to bolster the Saigon regime. Though the last U.S. combat troops had departed from Vietnam by February of 1973, approximately nine thousand Americans remained to act as advisors.

Nixon and Kissinger pressured Congress to provide further military aid to South Vietnam, asserting that it was essential to leave the Saigon regime in a good position to negotiate with the Communists should it become necessary. But, by this time, Congress was eager to totally extricate the United States from Vietnam, reflecting the overwhelmingly anti-Vietnam stance of its constituents. In addition, evidence that the Nixon administration had deliberately misled and even lied to Congress about U.S. activity in Southeast Asia made Congress even more defiant.

In July of 1973, Congress passed the War Powers Resolution, which stated that in the future, the president must report to Congress within forty-eight hours of (1) committing U.S. forces to a foreign conflict or (2) substantially increasing the number of combat troops in a foreign country. If Congress did not approve of the action within sixty days, the commitment would have to be terminated.

By the time the War Powers Act was signed into law in November, Nixon's influence on Congress had been greatly weakened by his involvement in the Watergate scandal (see Chapter 4), and Congress was growing increasingly assertive on the issue of Vietnam. Though Nixon had assured Thieu that the U.S. would intervene should the Communists attempt to overrun South Vietnam, Congress aimed to prevent that possibility through laws forbidding the use of military force anywhere in Southeast Asia. From 1973 to 1974, direct aid from the United States to South Vietnam was more than halved, and an already weak Saigon government began to crumble.

The Fall of Saigon

As aid from the U.S. dwindled and the economy in Saigon appeared to be collapsing, the North Vietnamese grew more and more confident that they would achieve their long-held goal of a Vietnam united under Communist rule. With the resignation of Richard Nixon in August of 1974, the U.S. military threat appeared more distant than ever, for Congress felt no obligation

VIETNAM WAR

For further information see primary source entries on pages

12: 1638-43, 1660-63

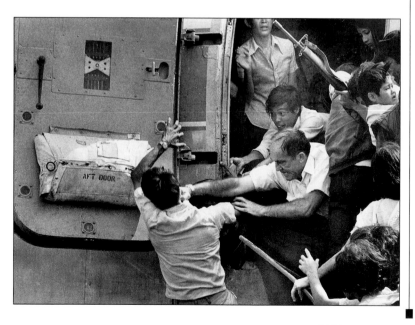

Desperation and panic seized the people of South Vietnam as the Communists invaded in April, 1975. Here a man tries to board an already overloaded refugee plane and is punched in the face by an American official.

to follow through on Nixon's promise to back up President Thieu.

In January of 1975, the North Vietnamese began a massive invasion of South Vietnam. The Communists quickly moved south, overwhelming the poorly prepared and sometimes leaderless South Vietnamese troops. As the North Vietnamese pushed on, Kissinger appealed to Congress for emergency aid to reinforce Saigon, but Congress refused.

By late March, panic was spreading like wildfire through South Vietnam, as hundreds of thousands of desperate refugees attempted to escape the bombs and advancing troops. Soon after the Communists began shelling Saigon, the last remaining South Vietnamese soldiers, realizing their certain fate if they stayed to fight, joined the fleeing throngs. Meanwhile, the U.S. was planning the emergency evacuation from Saigon of the remaining Americans and South Vietnamese citizens who had worked for American

agencies. With the Saigon airport under attack, the only alternative was to launch the largest helicopter evacuation ever attempted. On April 29, Operation Frequent Wind began. For the next eighteen hours, a fleet of seventy helicopters flew back and forth between the capital and the aircraft carriers positioned offshore. Over a thousand Americans and almost six thousand Vietnamese were airlifted out of Saigon. Just hours after the last American helicopters left for good on April 30, 1975, the South Vietnamese government surrendered to the North Vietnamese Army. Despite Nixon's claims that the U.S. had made an honorable exit from the war, to many Americans their country appeared anything but honorable.

During the next several years, as many as a million Vietnamese sought to escape the brutal oppression of Communist rule in rickety vessels bound for Thailand or other nearby countries. Thousands eventually arrived in the United States. The

Vietnamese refugees on a ship in Manila Bay in 1979. Four years after the Communists overran Vietnam, people were still trying to escape the country, often in flimsier vessels than the one shown here.

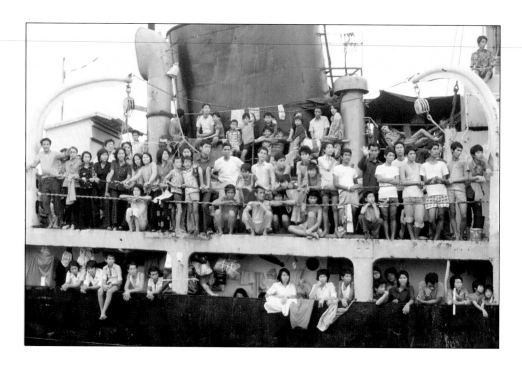

Haing Ngor. (1940-1996)

Though Cambodia was a poor country by Western standards, Haing Ngor came from a wealthy family. In the early seventies, life was going well for Ngor. After seven years of medical school, he had opened his own medical clinic in Phnom Penh, the capital of Cambodia, and he even drove a Mercedes.

But just a few months after Ngor was awarded his degree in obstetrics, the Khmer Rouge took over, and Ngor's life turned into a nightmare. The Communists ordered everyone to evacuate the capital, marching them into the countryside, where they were forced to work in brutal labor camps. Ngor and his wife, a teacher, had to hide their pasts, for the Khmer Rouge were killing doctors and other professionals in their quest to start a "new society." Ngor risked his life by secretly serving as a doctor in the labor camps.

After working long days at hard labor, often with only watery rice to eat, Ngor and his family were forced to attend Communist brainwashing sessions until late at night. Under such harsh conditions, Ngor's weight dropped from 140 to 70 pounds, and he came close to death. He was also tortured three times. The first time, the Khmer Rouge chopped off part of his finger for stealing food. Others in his family suffered even worse fates. His parents and brothers were executed, and Ngor's emaciated wife died in his arms while trying to give birth.

With an iron will and a survivor's instinct, Ngor finally escaped with a niece to a refugee camp in Thailand in 1979. There he worked as a doctor in the refugee clinic for just over a year in exchange for permission to emigrate to the U.S. Though Ngor built a good life in Los Angeles, he was haunted by the incredible horrors he had lived through. He was determined to tell the world about the misery of Cambodia under the Khmer Rouge. In the early eighties, Ngor landed a role in a movie about the horrors of the atrocities in Cambodia called *The Killing Fields*, a wrenching depiction of those times, for which he would later receive an Academy Award.

---

plight of these desperate "boat people" filled U.S. headlines well into the late seventies, serving as a reminder of an ugly war that Americans were trying to forget.

Perhaps the worst horrors against humanity to take place in Southeast Asia occurred in Cambodia. Less than two weeks before the fall of Saigon, an eerily similar scene occurred in Cambodia when its capital, Phnom Penh, fell to the Communist Khmer Rouge. American embassy personnel had to be evacuated by helicopter from that capital as well. Once in power, the Khmer Rouge ominously declared its intentions to create a "new society" and pronounced the beginning of Communist rule "Year Zero." They then embarked on a

horrific campaign to eliminate everyone who posed a potential threat. By some estimates, as many as two million of its people, approximately a quarter of the population, died, making the "killing fields" of Cambodia an atrocity on the level of the Nazi Holocaust.

The Legacy of Vietnam

As Communist rule spread in Southeast Asia, Americans tried desperately to push Vietnam into the past and get on with the future. Nixon's successor, President Gerald Ford, gave voice to the hopes held by most of his fellow Americans in a speech given just a week before the fall of Saigon:

"Vietnam is still with us. It has created doubts about American judgment, about American credibility, about American power — not only at home, but throughout the world. It has poisoned our domestic debate. So we paid an exorbitant price for the decisions that were made in good faith and for good purpose."

Henry Kissinger, on the legacy of the Vietnam War

This child's North Vietnamese father was exposed to the chemical Agent Orange sprayed by U.S. forces during the Vietnam War. Children of those exposed to this defoliant sometimes were born with defects. Many American GIs and their children were also affected.

Today, Americans can regain the sense of pride that existed before Vietnam, but it cannot be achieved by refighting a war that is finished. . . . These events, tragic as they are, portend neither the end of the world nor of America's leadership in the world.

But national pride, once lost, is difficult to recover. The fact that a superpower like the United States was ultimately unable, for whatever reason, to defeat a Third World country in war was a severe blow to America's image. In addition, the pursuit of that war had deeply divided the American public, and their faith in government was greatly weakened.

Future foreign policy was, not surprisingly, also affected by the experience of the Vietnam War. "The Vietnam Syndrome" was the term coined to describe America's reluctance to get involved in any future foreign conflict unless victory was virtually assured.

On a personal level, the lasting effects of the war were undoubtedly most deeply felt by the returning veterans and their families. On top of the difficulties of readjusting to ordinary life after experiencing the unspeakable horrors of war, many Vietnam veterans felt shunned by their fellow Americans, as if their mere presence was a painful reminder of a shameful ordeal. Veteran John Kerry, later elected senator of Massachusetts, remembered waking up screaming from a nightmare while flying across the country shortly after his return home:

The other passengers moved away from me — a reaction I noticed more and more in the months ahead. . . . The feeling toward [returning vets] was, "Stay away — don't contaminate us with whatever you've brought back from Vietnam."

Statistics compiled during the decade after the war bear out the difficulties experienced by many Vietnam vets. The rates of alcoholism, drug addiction, divorce, crime, unemployment, and suicide are all much higher among veterans than they are for nonveterans.

In addition to the emotional and mental scars left by the Vietnam war, some vets and their offspring suffered serious health problems caused by exposure to Agent Orange, a weed and plant killer used extensively by the U.S. throughout most of the war. This powerful defoliant was dropped on many jungle areas to destroy the Communist guerrillas' protective cover and to deprive them of a food source. A great deal of evidence suggests that exposure to Agent Orange caused skin rashes, birth defects, and cancer.

While returned veterans struggled to get on with their lives, many Americans were deeply concerned about the men who did not come back from Vietnam. Soon after the signing of the peace pact, North Vietnam returned close to six hundred prisoners of war (POWs) to the United States. Most had been held in terrible conditions, some for seven years or longer. In prisons such as the "Hanoi Hilton," prisoners were often tortured or held in solitary confinement for extended periods.

Not including the returned POWs, over two thousand combatants were still listed as MIA, or missing in action. Most had been lost in battle or when their aircraft were downed, and so were presumed dead. Though many more men were lost in World War II and the Korean War, the public outcry over the MIAs in Vietnam was unprecedented. Perhaps it was the defeat of the United States in the Vietnam War that made the idea of soldiers missing in action so difficult to accept. In response to the protests, the administrations of both Gerald Ford and Jimmy Carter set up commissions to look into the issue. Though investigations revealed no evidence of live MIAs in Vietnam, anger and suspicion persisted. Many Americans remained convinced that the government was so eager to close the book on the Vietnam War that it

did not conduct a sufficiently thorough search for the missing men.

The public's distrust of its government on this issue is evidence of just one of the legacies of the Vietnam War. Another is the loss of 57,690 Americans who died in the conflict. Their names are listed on what is now the most visited attraction in Washington, D.C., the Vietnam War Memorial, commonly known as "The Wall." The Vietnam War still sparks angry debates among Americans, and it is still a strong influence on U.S. foreign policy. As Henry Kissinger put it, "Vietnam is still with us."

Vietnam veterans, photographed in 1986, pay their respects to those who died in the war at the Vietnam War Memorial in Washington D.C. In the background is a flag made of flowers, one for each American who died. Many veterans felt that other Americans found them an embarrassing reminder of a national ordeal they would rather forget.

CHAPTER 3
Nixon in the White House

> *"We are torn by division. To a crisis of the spirit, we need an answer of the spirit. And to find that answer, we need only look within ourselves . . . .We cannot learn from one another until we stop shouting at one another — until we speak quietly enough so that our words can be heard as well as our voices. For its part, government will listen."*
>
> Richard Nixon, in a 1968 inaugural speech

Togetherness versus Politics

The presidential election year of 1968 was a year of turmoil and tragedy. Both Martin Luther King, Jr., and Robert F. Kennedy were slain, the number of U.S. troops in Vietnam was near its highest point, and cities across the country erupted in riots. While out on the campaign trail, Richard Nixon noticed a sign that bore the poignant message, "Bring Us Together Again," and in his victory speech, Nixon announced that his goal would be just that, to "bring us together."

By 1970, however, that goal seemed to be fading into the background as other, more political ambitions took hold. When Nixon was elected, he promised that his administration would be "open to new ideas" and "open to men and women of both parties." Those were soothing words to a troubled nation. But the reality of party politics was not to be denied, and the Nixon administration soon set about constructing a strategy for consolidating Republican power in Washington and insuring Nixon's reelection. Part of that strategy was based on an important change occurring in the nation's demographics.

The Rise of the Sunbelt

In 1969, a political observer named Kevin Phillips published a book entitled *The Emerging Republican Majority*, which was to have an important influence on the Nixon administration. In it, Phillips coined a term that would quickly catch on — the Sunbelt. Though the exact boundaries of the Sunbelt are often debated, most people agree that it incorporates the states along the southern rim of the country. The Sunbelt had been experiencing a rapid population growth since World War II, and that growth was especially noticeable in the seventies. In 1976, the Census Bureau reported that the metropolitan areas of the South and Southwest were the only ones experiencing substantial population growth since 1970. This influx of people to the South signaled the reversal of a trend that had lasted about a hundred years — the migration of people (especially African-Americans and young people) to the North in search of a better life.

A combination of factors induced more and more people to move south after World War II. The warmer weather of the region held a strong appeal to northerners, especially once the widespread use of air conditioners made excessive heat and humidity less of a problem. Florida and Arizona became common destinations for retirees looking for an easier lifestyle in their golden years.

Economic factors also played an important role. The economy entered a recession in the seventies, and unemployment was high throughout much of the nation. But the defense, high technology, and aerospace industries, which were centered in the South and the Sunbelt, were creating new jobs. In addition, the oil embargo of 1973 was a boon to oil- and gas-producing states such as Texas and Louisiana. Houston, Texas, is an excellent example of a southern city whose population exploded in the seventies, fueled in large part by the booming oil industry. Between 1970 and 1980, the population of Houston and its surrounding suburbs grew by almost one million people, an increase of 44.6 percent.

What does the rise of the Sunbelt have to do with politics? The increase in population meant that the South/Sunbelt was gaining electoral power, and Kevin Phillips argued that the Republicans were likely to be the beneficiaries. Many of the people moving to the Sunbelt were white, middle- to upper-class citizens who were more likely to vote Republican. In addition, many traditional southern Democrats were growing frustrated with the liberal spending policies of the Democrats.

The people who had voted for George Wallace in the 1968 election were yet another important Southern group for the Republicans. As a presidential candidate, Wallace combined racism hidden in code words with a militant, law-and-order theme. Wallace attracted many conservative southern voters who sought to voice their protest about the direction the country was taking. The three-way race made for a close election, and Nixon won with only 43 percent of the vote. Attorney General John Mitchell believed that in order to win in 1972, the president would have to

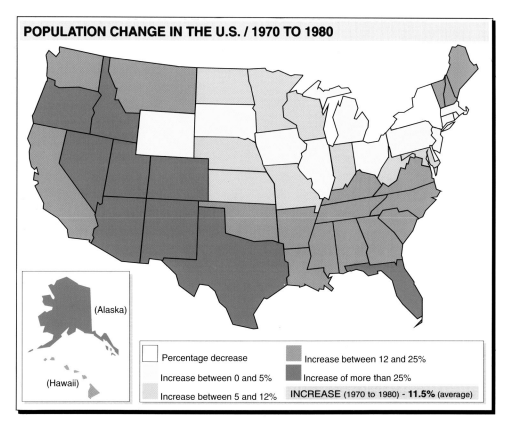

POPULATION CHANGE IN THE U.S. / 1970 TO 1980

(Alaska)

(Hawaii)

Percentage decrease

Increase between 0 and 5%

Increase between 5 and 12%

Increase between 12 and 25%

Increase of more than 25%

INCREASE (1970 to 1980) - **11.5%** (average)

This map shows the percentage increase in the population of each state in the U.S. between 1970 and 1980. The most dramatic increases were in the Sunbelt states of the South and Southwest. Here, new jobs in high technology industries were created and more people retired to the South because of the warmer climate.

Houston's steel and glass skyline rises above the prairie, a reflection of the importance of the oil industry. Oil and gas producing southern states boomed after the 1973 Arab oil embargo.

lure the people who voted for George Wallace in 1968. He therefore promoted the "southern strategy," which was based on the premise that the Nixon administration must avoid making any moves that would antagonize conservative southerners.

Of course, the idea behind this strategy was not to bring Americans together, but rather to divide them. By trying to win the support of Wallace voters, Nixon was sure to antagonize civil rights advocates, and by appealing to the law-and-order vote, he would even further alienate the youth movement. Apparently these were risks that Nixon was willing to take.

Southern Strategy and the Supreme Court

Part of Attorney General Mitchell's strategy was to repay southern Republicans for the role they played in nominating Nixon at the 1968 National Republican Convention. So, when two Supreme Court seats opened up in 1969, Nixon promised to try to fill the vacancies with "strict constructionists" who would advocate a narrow, literal interpretation of the Constitution. This promise was a direct appeal to southerners and conservatives, who resented the civil rights decisions handed down by the Supreme Court in the past two decades.

Nixon's first nominee, Warren Burger, was confirmed without trouble. For the next seat, Nixon wanted a white, southern conservative. He chose Judge Clement F. Haynsworth, Jr., of South Carolina. He was rejected by the Senate in November of 1969, after opponents portrayed him as antilabor and indifferent to civil rights. Nixon was infuriated and defiant at news of the rejection. Rather than seek a moderate nominee who would be acceptable to the majority in Congress, the president was more determined then ever to name a conservative southerner to the Supreme Court. On January 19, 1970, Nixon nominated G. Harrold Carswell of Tallahassee, Florida. It was a move he would soon regret.

In the haste to find a suitable candidate, Carswell's past had not been thoroughly checked, and once he was nominated, this history became the subject of great controversy. To begin with, the legal community loudly decried Carswell as being unqualified for a position on the Supreme Court. Then the story came out that the judge had given a speech in 1948 declaring his belief in white supremacy. Despite lobbying efforts by the White House, the Senate rejected Carswell's nomination.

The man finally confirmed to the Supreme Court seat was Harry Blackmun. He was regarded as a fair-minded, scholarly judge, and his nomination was quickly confirmed.

The nomination battles were highly divisive, but in the South, Nixon's image was enhanced among the former Wallace supporters.

Nixon and the Youth Movement

While the South was warming up to Nixon, members of the youth movement saw him as the embodiment of everything they hated. The president wavered in his response to them. On the one hand, he refused to be pushed around by student demonstrators, but at times, he felt the need to appease young voters. Nixon's personality, however, was not conducive to winning over young people. He often seemed aloof and awkward, and Nixon himself acknowledged his lack of charm. The hard-line, law-and-order rhetoric coming from the White House did nothing to soften his image among students. Responding to the Kent State tragedy in Ohio, White House press secretary Ron Ziegler said the killings "should remind us all once again that when dissent turns to violence it invites tragedy." Young Americans were outraged by this statement, which appeared to blame

"I understand the bitter feelings of millions of Americans who live in the South. They have my assurance that the day will come when judges like Carswell and Haynsworth can and will sit on the High Court."

Richard Nixon

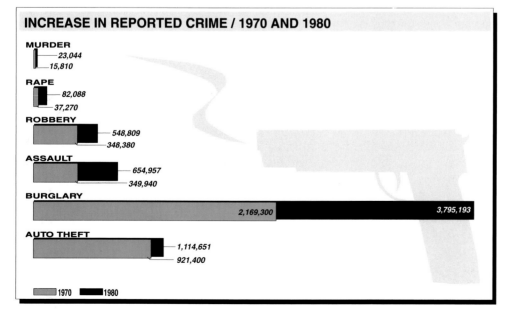

INCREASE IN REPORTED CRIME / 1970 AND 1980

MURDER
23,044
15,810

RAPE
82,088
37,270

ROBBERY
548,809
348,380

ASSAULT
654,957
349,940

BURGLARY
2,169,300   3,795,193

AUTO THEFT
1,114,651
921,400

1970   1980

This chart shows that all categories of crimes increased dramatically between 1970 and 1980, despite the promise of Nixon and his administration to give priority to law and order.

the four students for their own deaths.

As campuses across the country were racked by student unrest, the president began rethinking his tough stance. In the early morning hours of May 9, 1970, a hundred thousand young antiwar demonstrators were gathering in Washington to protest the Kent State massacre. On an impulse, Nixon made a visit to the Lincoln Memorial to talk to some of the students. In the conversations that followed, Nixon discussed the social issues of the day, made small talk, and tried to get across one important message regarding the war: "Remember,

I feel just as deeply as you do about this," he said. Unfortunately for Nixon, his efforts backfired. Students only expressed their dismay at the president's irrelevant small talk when they obviously had much more pressing issues on their minds.

The 1970 Election and the Politics of Fear

The student protesters were not the only bur under Nixon's saddle. He was also tormented by a hostile Congress that blocked many of the

Vice President Spiro Agnew relished using strong and colorful language to accuse the Democrats of supporting liberalism and permissive behavior.

programs and legislation coming from the White House. As the midterm congressional elections of 1970 approached, however, the Nixon administration had hopes that a friendlier Congress could be seated. In fact, Nixon's supporters had more than hopes: They had a strategy.

The plan was to pin all of the social ills affecting voters — drugs, crime, and campus unrest — on the "permissive" atmosphere created by Democrats in government. In addition, Nixon hoped to further split the already divided Democratic party by forcing Democratic candidates to either embrace the most liberal elements of their party or reject them.

Nixon decided that the person who should be most responsible for putting the Democrats on the defensive was his vice president, Spiro T. Agnew. A staunch conservative, Agnew relished the role. He crisscrossed the nation, appearing at Republican fundraisers to deliver his stinging diatribes. When critics tried to bring the issues of inflation and the lingering war into the campaign, Agnew counter-attacked, calling them "nattering nabobs of negativism."

The strategy seemed to be working and the Democrats were on the run, but as the campaign wore on, people grew tired of the tough messages. Then an odd series of events caused the momentum to swing in the Democrats' favor. After the president spoke to a group of five thousand supporters in San Jose, California, his motorcade was pelted with rocks and eggs by a group of hostile protesters who gathered outside the hall.

A few days later, on election eve, Nixon decided to forego the usual, cool-tempered speech. Instead, he chose to broadcast on television a speech he had given at a campaign stop in response to the San Jose incident. In the speech, the president referred to the demonstrators as "haters" and said there was a difference between freedom of speech and rock throwing. As for the antiwar protesters, Nixon said, "Those who carry a peace sign in one hand and throw a bomb or a brick with another are the super hypocrites of our time." Though the speech had been well received earlier, it was not the proper tone for election eve. Immediately following Nixon, Democratic Senator Edmund Muskie spoke, calmly urging Americans to not give in to the "politics of fear." The Republicans failed to win a majority in either the House or the Senate.

Indecision and the Domestic Agenda

Nixon had come into office promising to reverse the trend of big government and roll back the costly Great Society programs begun under the Johnson administration. But beyond that, Nixon did not have a real theme for his domestic policy. Though the president enjoyed the strategy of international affairs, he lacked focus and conviction when it came to the domestic agenda.

One of Nixon's goals was welfare reform. Though Johnson's war on poverty was hailed as a great plan at first, by 1970 many were disillusioned by the results. Critics claimed that welfare encouraged people to remain unemployed rather than work at available, low-paying jobs. More and more people were also complaining about what the high cost of welfare programs

"Will Americans be led by a president elected by a majority of the American people or will we be intimidated and blackmailed into following the path dictated by a disruptive and militant minority — the pampered prodigies of the radical liberals in the United States Senate?"

Vice President Spiro Agnew, 1970 campaign speech

> *"You say to the cities, now look here — here's the money . . . .We're saying to you 'you know best.' If your property taxes are too high, and you want to cut back on Great Society programs, you can."*
>
> Richard Nixon, to his Domestic Council

was doing to taxes. In response, the Nixon administration proposed the Family Assistance Plan, a program that would make welfare more equitable nationwide and also encourage recipients to work. Though the plan was innovative in many ways, liberals said that it did not provide enough help for the poor, and conservatives complained that it would not really bring about reform. Ultimately, the plan was doomed and failed in Congress.

The other main element of Nixon's domestic program fared better. Entitled "the New Federalism," the program aimed to return power to the states. Under Johnson's Great Society approach, the federal government had taken on a great deal of social authority. Nixon was highly critical of this trend for three reasons: (1) It was very costly; (2) it was mired in bureaucracy; and (3) he felt that it undermined the sense of community and the authority of state and local governments to effectively deal with regional problems. To reverse this trend, Nixon proposed a "revenue-sharing" policy. Simply put, the federal government would give grants directly to state and local governments to be spent as they saw fit. Though liberals worried that important Great Society programs would be cut back, Nixon correctly gauged the mood of the public, and the revenue-sharing plan was passed in Congress.

A Dark Cloud Over the Economy

While Nixon was preoccupied with bringing an end to the war in Vietnam, troubles were brewing at home on the economic front. Not only was inflation on the rise, but the country appeared to be heading into a recession. Productivity was down and interest rates were climbing, while business leaders and consumers alike called on the president to *do something.*

Nixon had little interest in economics. He was therefore happy to find someone who could liven up what was to him a dull subject. John Connally, former Democratic governor of Texas, was a colorful, outgoing character prone to taking risks. In 1970, Nixon appointed Connally secretary of the treasury. One year later, with the economic situation worsening, Nixon called a meeting to discuss what to do. With characteristic boldness, Connally suggested a plan that would grab the attention of the American public and the international community as well. The Nixon administration had promised a hands-off approach to the free-market economy, but at this point, Connally believed, it was time for the government to intervene.

On August 15, 1971, Nixon announced on television his New Economic Policy. The most dramatic part of the plan was a ninety-day freeze on prices, wages, and rents. In addition, Nixon announced a 10 percent border tax to cut down competition from imports, and he closed the "gold window" to stop the devaluation of the dollar on the international market. Overall, the public reaction was good. People were happy the president was taking action. But in retrospect, Nixon would regret his efforts to exert such strong controls on the economy. While the wage and price freeze did temporarily help, once the controls were lifted, inflation skyrocketed.

But the worst damage to the U.S. economy was caused by a war being fought half-way around the world. In October of 1973, Egyptian and Syrian troops crossed into Israeli-occupied territory, signaling the beginning of the Yom Kippur War. When the U.S. announced it was sending a large package of military aid to Israel, Arab nations began an oil embargo against the United States and other nations deemed "friendly" to Israel. The Arab countries subsequently formed the Organization of Petroleum Exporting Countries (OPEC) to set production levels and international oil prices. Before the embargo was lifted in 1974, the cost of oil had more than quadrupled, sending shock waves throughout the economy. Inflation rose sharply in most industrialized nations. The West was quickly learning all about the power of oil.

As prices at the gas pump skyrocketed, Japanese economy cars, which were known for their good gas mileage, became more attractive to American consumers. The popularity of Japanese cars was one cause of a problem that was quietly growing — the trade deficit. Japan was quickly becoming America's chief economic rival by producing inexpensive, quality goods

Israeli tanks head towards Damascus, Syria, in October 1973. Secretary of State Henry Kissinger tried for two years without success to negotiate a lasting peace in the Middle East.

Traffic chaos ensues as Chicago motorists line up for gas in early 1974. A group of Arab nations began an oil embargo against countries that supported Israel in the 1973 Yom Kippur War. The effect of this was that oil prices increased dramatically. President Nixon refused to consider rationing fuel or any long-term policy to conserve energy resources.

(especially cars and electronics) and aggressively exporting those goods while protecting their own domestic industries from imports. Other Asian nations were also silently becoming economic powerhouses. As Congressman Don Bonker noted, "Though few Americans seemed to notice, the U.S. was on its way to changing from the world's largest creditor nation to the world's largest debtor nation."

The Right Time for Détente

While the picture on the economic scene looked rather bleak, Nixon and his national security advisor, Henry Kissinger, were setting the stage for dramatic developments in foreign affairs. Though Nixon was known as a tough anticommunist, years of an escalating arms race and

dangerous episodes of teetering on the edge of international war between the superpowers had convinced him that the future safety of the world could only be assured by pursuing a path of negotiation instead of confrontation. Nixon's overarching goal in foreign policy would be summed up in one word — détente, which means the easing of discord between nations.

Nixon and Kissinger sensed that the time was right for approaching both China and the Soviet Union. The Soviet Union and the U.S. had reached a level of relative parity in the arms race, which meant they were both in a position to negotiate. In addition, relations between the USSR and China were growing increasingly tense, with troops amassing along their common border. In the competition for power between the two Communist giants, Nixon saw the opportunity to play one off against the other. He calculated that both countries would be eager to improve their world status and therefore each would want to be on better terms with the U.S. than the other.

Another factor that made the timing seem right for détente was the feeling that only Nixon could get away with approaching the Communist nations. After many years of taking a tough stance against Communists, Americans could feel secure that Nixon would not "give away the store" in negotiations. And while rightwingers would surely scream if a Kennedy or a Johnson made concessions to the Communists, they would be more hesitant to loudly criticize one of their own.

Henry Kissinger played an essential role in the delicate maneuvering toward détente, and in the process, he gained superstar status in the U.S. and abroad. A former Harvard professor, Kissinger possessed a commanding

intellect and quickly became adept at the power game. Like Nixon, he hated bureaucracy. In collusion with the president, he worked outside the State Department, often without the knowledge even of Secretary of State William Rogers.

Parting the Bamboo Curtain: Nixon's Trip to China

Richard Nixon had long been fascinated with China. In 1949, when the Nationalist Chinese government was overthrown by the Communists, Nixon denounced the Truman administration for "losing China." Ever since that time, the U.S. had recognized the island of Taiwan, to which Nationalist Chinese officials had fled after the revolution, as the legitimate seat of Chinese government, while isolating

COMMUNISM

For further information see primary source entries on pages

11: 1511-13, 1571-82;
12: 1596-1602, 1605-11

The U.S. table tennis team visited China in April 1971 as part of the diplomatic effort to achieve better relations between the two countries, giving rise to the term "ping-pong diplomacy."

President Nixon in China, February 1973. The trip marked the end of almost twenty-five years of hostility between the two countries. Earlier, the U.S. had vetoed China's entry to the United Nations and had instead recognized Taiwan as the true seat of Chinese government. Now Nixon wanted to open up new markets for American products, and the Chinese wanted U.S. friendship as security against the Soviet Union.

mainland China from the Western world. By now, however, Nixon realized that the Communist government was firmly entrenched and would probably remain so for some time to come. He also realized that China was too important to be excluded from, as he put it, "the family of nations." It was time, Nixon decided, to end almost twenty-five years of antagonism between the two countries.

Nixon began making overtures to China by, among other things, easing travel and trade restrictions. Then, in April of 1971, China surprised everyone by inviting the American table tennis team to visit China, where they were warmly received, and the U.S., in turn, extended an invitation to the Chinese team. After this episode of "ping-pong diplomacy," Kissinger made a secret trip to Beijing. The story was put out that he had fallen ill while traveling through Asia and had taken to his bed. In reality, Kissinger was laying the groundwork for the first visit ever by a United States president to the People's Republic of China.

Nixon compared his planned trip to the *Apollo 11* flight, referring to the plaque the astronauts left on the moon, which says, "We came in peace for all mankind." Just before finally embarking on his journey, the president further explained his mission to a group gathered at the White House:

We must recognize that the government of the People's Republic of China and the government of the United States have had great differences. We will have differences in the future. But what we must do is to find a way to see that we can have differences without being enemies in war.

Realizing the historical importance of the trip, and with an eye toward upcoming presidential elections, the White House did all it could to maximize positive media coverage of the event. During the president's week in China, from February 21-29, 1972, he was followed by mobs of American television crews and reporters as he visited the Great Wall, attended banquets, and toured the Forbidden City in Beijing.

At the end of the week, Nixon and Chinese Premier Chou Enlai issued a joint statement, called the Shanghai Communiqué. The crux of the communiqué was that both nations agreed on the need to increase contacts between them. There was, however, a controversial element to the communiqué. In one passage, the U.S. recognized that Taiwan was part of China and stated its objective to ultimately withdraw all U.S. military forces from Taiwan. Critics on the right assailed the president for giving up on Taiwan, but to Nixon and Kissinger, the agreement was an essential step toward détente.

The Moscow Summit

Just three months after his return from China, Nixon embarked on another historic trip. On May 22, 1972, he became the first United States president to visit Moscow. As dramatic as was the opening of China, Nixon hoped to reach more substantial agreements with the Soviet Union that would result in a safer world. For two and one-half years, the United States and the Soviet Union had been engaged in Strategic Arms Limitation Talks (SALT), and though a general framework for agreement had been established, important differences remained. Nixon and Kissinger hoped to resolve those differences in Moscow and return home with a signed treaty that would be an important first step in controlling nuclear weapons.

However, some observers feared that the Moscow summit would be over before it began. Shortly before Nixon was to leave for Moscow, he ordered the mining of Haiphong harbor and renewed bombing in North Vietnam. Though North Vietnam was a Soviet ally and the USSR had been supplying them with military aid

"Everywhere, new hopes are rising for a world no longer overshadowed by fear, and want, and war."

Richard Nixon, on the signing of the SALT agreement

throughout the war, the Kremlin (the seat of government of the USSR) issued a relatively mild statement condemning the bombing. The fact that they did not call off the summit indicated to Nixon and Kissinger that the Soviets wanted an agreement just as badly as the U.S. did.

In May 1972, President Nixon and Soviet leader Leonid Brezhnev signed an arms agreement that limited or froze the number of nuclear weapons on both sides. As a result of his two foreign visits, Nixon's popularity at home rose, helping him to an election victory later the same year.

To get the summit off to a good start, several prearranged agreements were signed amid ceremonial splendor. The agreements provided for cooperation in areas including science, medical research, space exploration, and environmental study. But the crowning glory of the summit came when President Nixon and Soviet leader Leonid Brezhnev signed the SALT accords, which limited the deployment of defensive systems and froze the number of offensive weapons on both sides. The agreement was based on the premise that the nuclear weapons of both superpowers had created a "balance of terror" that restrained them from entering into an all-out war.

A few weeks after the summit, in an attempt to develop better economic relations with the Soviets, the U.S. agreed to sell them at least $750 million in American grain over a three-year period. Because the Soviets ended up buying nearly a billion dollars' worth of grain in the first year, the increased demand led to high inflation in the American food market.

But this troublesome side-effect of the summit was off in the future. As the summit came to a close, Nixon was euphoric, and except for the hard-line conservatives back home, the reaction of the American public was overwhelmingly positive. The timing, of course, could not have been better. With the presidential election just around the corner, Nixon had scored two important foreign policy triumphs. With the opening of China and the signing of SALT, the world seemed a safer place. Despite his conduct in the Vietnam War, Nixon was setting himself up as the "peace president." By confidently handling the delicate maneuvers toward détente, Nixon had, as his speech writer William Safire put it, "shown himself to be the kind of person one would hope to see as President of the United States."

But what would be the long-term effect of détente on American foreign policy? Would the balance of power between the United States, China, and the Soviet Union be maintained? Ultimately, Nixon did not have the chance to test his policy, for his second term was to be cut short by the Watergate scandal.

CHAPTER 4
The Watergate Affair

① The Seeds of Destruction

As the presidential election of 1972 drew near, Nixon appeared stronger than ever. He had lessened the threat of nuclear war, he had brought home almost all of the troops from Vietnam, and he was managing to stimulate the economy by pumping up federal spending. On top of all that, the Democrats were about to nominate a comparatively weak candidate, South Dakota Senator George McGovern, to run against him.

But Nixon was never one to take a political victory for granted. His narrow defeat by John F. Kennedy in the 1960 presidential election and his unsuccessful bid to be governor of California in 1962 were still bitter memories. Those experiences taught Nixon how instrumental the press could be in influencing an election's outcome. Nixon had always felt unfairly treated by members of the media, believing they were dominated by a liberal bias. He described the press as "unelected members of the elite" and considered them the

Nixon in a campaign motorcade in October 1972. Despite his obvious strength going into the election, Nixon and his supporters were worried enough to instigate bugging and wiretapping in the Democratic party headquarters. It would take two years for all the facts of this scandal to be made public and force the president to resign.

enemy. Another factor that concerned Nixon was the antiwar movement, which, though quieter than before, still had the potential to dis-

G. Gordon Liddy (left), the ex-FBI agent who suggested bugging the Watergate complex, went on trial with others in January 1973. Five of the accused pleaded guilty, raising suspicions of a cover-up. Here, in a later case, Liddy is charged with conspiracy and burglary of the offices of Daniel Ellsberg, who leaked the Pentagon Papers *to the press.*

rupt his reelection campaign as long as Americans were in Vietnam.

As shown earlier, Nixon's hatred of the press and concern over antiwar dissenters led to the creation of a secret unit known as the "plumbers," whose job it was to plug press leaks. As the election approached and the pressure was on to ensure a victory, the plumbers turned their attention to the Democratic opponents. One of the most enthusiastic plumbers was

G. Gordon Liddy, an ex-FBI agent. In January of 1972, Liddy reportedly met with several members of Nixon's staff, including Attorney General John Mitchell, who was about to leave the administration to become Nixon's campaign director. Liddy was said to have presented an elaborate plan to thwart the Democrats that included electronic surveillance and even kidnapping teams. Mitchell allegedly rejected the more bizarre elements of the plan, but approved the electronic surveillance idea.

The Break-in

At 2:30 A.M. on the morning of June 17, 1972, five men were arrested in the headquarters of the Democratic National Committee, located at the Watergate, a plush hotel/apartment complex in Washington, D.C. The men were wearing rubber gloves and carried wiretapping and bugging equipment. There could be little doubt why they were there. One of the men, James McCord, was employed by the Committee to Re-Elect the President (CRP, or "CREEP," as it would later be called), and two of the burglars were linked to a former White House consultant named E. Howard Hunt, Jr. Democratic National Chairman Lawrence O'Brien called the break-in a "blatant act of political espionage" and announced that his party was filing a civil lawsuit against the CRP. He also called for an FBI investigation.

At first, the public was shocked by the news, but the White House immediately denied any involvement and the story gradually faded from the headlines. Meanwhile, however, a federal grand jury was conducting a

Bob Woodward and Carl Bernstein.

Barely acquainted before the Watergate story, Woodward and Bernstein came from very different backgrounds. Woodward was a Yale graduate who spent several years in the navy, while Bernstein was the son of Communists and a college dropout. But after Watergate, their names would be forever linked.

Woodward was working the police beat for the *Washington Post* when he was called to cover the Watergate break-in. Bernstein followed up with a story about the burglars. From then on, they worked together, trying to uncover the money trail from the Committee to Re-Elect the President to the burglars. They doggedly searched for pieces of the puzzle, interviewing former employees of the CRP and anyone else who might know something. Through their investigations, they discovered an organized campaign of political sabotage linked to the CRP.

Woodward and Bernstein kept most of their sources confidential, but their editors insisted on confirmation from a second source for each alleged fact. Woodward's most valuable source was a high-ranking White House insider, whose identity was not revealed even to the editors. Woodward often met with this source, who went by the code name "Deep Throat," in the middle of the night at an underground garage. Speculation still continues about the true identity of Deep Throat.

For nine months, Woodward and Bernstein were virtually the only reporters covering Watergate. Some of the reporters' investigative tactics were criticized as unethical, such as gaining access to confidential phone and credit records and approaching members of the grand jury. Their stories were regularly attacked by the White House as "shoddy journalism" and "based on hearsay." But "Woodstein" sometimes discovered information even before the FBI or the grand jury investigations did. Woodward and Bernstein's stories prodded along the official investigations and eventually led to the downfall of the president. They also inspired a surge in investigative journalism.

In 1974, Woodward and Bernstein wrote a book about their experience uncovering Watergate, called *All the President's Men*, which they followed up with another entitled *The Final Days*, about the last months of the Nixon presidency. Both were immediate bestsellers.

Bob Woodward (left) and Carl Bernstein at their Washington Post *desk.*

secret investigation, and two diligent reporters from the *Washington Post*, Bob Woodward and Carl Bernstein, continued digging for information. In August of 1972, Woodward and Bernstein put Watergate back in the news by reporting evidence that the CRP had a secret fund used to pay for a "dirty tricks" campaign against the Democrats — dirty tricks that included the Watergate break-in. The story consumed the attention of the two reporters for the next two years and turned them into household names. Their report led to a flurry of speculation about how high the scandal would go. At this point, however, only the most cynical believed it would lead all the way to the top — the president himself.

③ **The Cover-up**

Shortly after the Watergate burglars were arrested, three of Nixon's top aides, H. R. Haldeman, John Ehrlichman, and John Dean, took swift action to cover up White House involvement in the break-in. Documents were destroyed, Hunt's White House safe was emptied, and, on June 23, 1972, Haldeman had a very important meeting with the president. He explained to Nixon that if the FBI investigation continued, it could turn up very damaging information linking the burglars directly to the CRP. Nixon and Haldeman decided to tell the FBI that it was on the verge of revealing information that would embarrass the CIA and that the investigation should therefore be halted. Though Nixon did not realize it at the time, he had just made a fatal mistake.

But the burglars themselves still posed a serious problem. If they began naming names, the implications could be disastrous for the White House. Through clandestine channels, several members of Nixon's staff arranged to pay "hush money" to the burglars and held out the promise that they would be granted clemency if they pleaded guilty.

④ **The 1972 Election**

Ironically, Nixon's lead in the 1972 campaign was so great that the plumbers' activities, besides being illegal, were totally unnecessary. There was really no need to sabotage the Democratic campaign since the Democrats themselves were doing a fine job of spoiling their own

chances for victory. Many political observers say that George McGovern's campaign was undermined right at the start of the Democratic National Convention.

After the disastrous 1968 convention, McGovern and other Democratic leaders instituted reforms that led to a better representation of women, African-Americans, and other minorities at the 1972 convention. Young people were also better represented, and were an important group since the voting age had recently been lowered from twenty-one to eighteen. To those long excluded from the convention process, the diversity of delegates represented a great success, but many people watching the nationally televised proceedings saw things differently. Mainstream Democrats were offended by delegates speaking out for homosexual rights, abortion rights, amnesty for draft dodgers and deserters, and other controversial positions. Though McGovern's acceptance speech was more moderate, it was not broadcast until 3:00 A.M., after most viewers were long asleep. However erroneously, many voters associated McGovern's campaign with the radical left and feared that if McGovern were elected, it might mean a return to the turmoil of the late sixties.

Another serious blow to George McGovern's campaign involved his vice-presidential candidate, Thomas Eagleton. After his nomination, reporters discovered that Eagleton had been hospitalized three times for psychiatric disorders. At first, McGovern pledged that he was "1,000 percent for Tom Eagleton," despite the revelations. But soon he bowed to pressure and asked Eagleton to withdraw from the ticket. This sudden change

---

"I can categorically say that no one on the present White House staff, no one in this administration, was involved in this very bizarre incident."

Richard Nixon

WATERGATE

For further information see primary source entries on pages

12: 1673-80

George McGovern.

As senator from South Dakota during the Kennedy and Johnson administrations, George McGovern acquired a reputation as a liberal for his strong support of civil rights and social welfare programs, and for his vocal opposition to the Vietnam War. When Nixon was elected president, McGovern quickly became one of his strongest critics in the Senate. He dismissed the Nixon administration's Vietnamization policy as a "political hoax" and attacked Nixon for ordering a blockade of Haiphong harbor in North Vietnam without consulting Congress. "He's behaving more like a king, acting from divine right, than the leader of a free society," McGovern said of the president.

When McGovern announced he was running as a Democratic candidate in the 1972 presidential election, most political critics thought he had little chance of winning the nomination because he was considered too radical. But the Democratic party was divided, and reforms in the delegate selection process (which McGovern helped institute) led to a greater number of African-Americans, women, and young people at the National Convention, many of whom supported McGovern.

Though he won the nomination, McGovern's campaign was weak. His tax and welfare proposals were considered too extreme by many, including Democratic candidate Hubert Humphrey, who said McGovern was out to "revolutionize the country by massive redistribution of wealth." Critics also claimed that McGovern's plans for cutting defense spending would leave the United States too vulnerable. In addition, McGovern's strongest campaign issue, opposition to the Vietnam War, lost its impact when Kissinger announced shortly before the election that peace was at hand. McGovern lost the election, carrying only Massachusetts and the District of Columbia.

In 1974, McGovern was reelected to a third term in the Senate. There he continued to fight for one of his favorite causes — ending hunger in the U.S. He fought off attempts to weaken the food stamp plan and pushed for higher spending on school lunch programs. In the late seventies, he found himself battling a president from his own party when Jimmy Carter proposed cuts in welfare programs and increases in defense spending.

of heart deeply hurt George McGovern's image.

As if things weren't bad enough, just weeks before the election, Henry Kissinger told reporters that peace was near in Vietnam. Though Kissinger's statement would later be proven untrue, it effectively stole the thunder from McGovern's main campaign promise — to immediately withdraw all U.S. troops from Vietnam.

When the last ballots were counted, Nixon had won by a landslide with 60.7 percent of the popular vote, carrying every state in the union but one. Though the president's family and staff were elated, Nixon himself was subdued. Despite the mandate

> *"Every tree in the forest will fall."*
>
> James McCord,
> Watergate burglar

John Dean, a Nixon aide, at first covered up White House involvement in the Watergate break-in, but in mid-1973, he began to cooperate with federal prosecutors in an attempt to avoid a prison sentence.

he had received, Richard Nixon was deeply troubled by two problems he could not seem to shake off: Vietnam and Watergate.

The Beginning of the Blow-up

As the Watergate scandal slowly unfolded, Nixon and his top aides, Haldeman, Ehrlichman, and Dean, met on several occasions to discuss how to proceed. At times, the idea of coming clean, or going "the hang-out road," as Nixon put it, was discussed. But everyone seemed to agree that road was too dangerous. Instead, Nixon and his aides decided on a strategy that would treat the scandal as a public relations problem. They reasoned that as long as Nixon gave the appearance of cooperating with the investigations, the American people would be satisfied. But this strategy was bound to fail. Nixon and his aides had not only overestimated the gullibility of the American public, they had also overestimated their ability to control the cover-up.

In January of 1973, the Watergate burglars went on trial along with Howard Hunt and G. Gordon Liddy, who allegedly ordered the break-in. Presiding over the case was a hard-nosed judge named John J. Sirica. When five of the accused pleaded guilty, Sirica was immediately suspicious that the defendants were involved in a cover-up. His suspicions were confirmed when McCord wrote a letter to the judge, charging that the other defendants had been pressured to plead guilty and that the orders for the break-in had come from people "higher up" than Hunt and Liddy.

A few months later, Nixon learned of an even greater threat. John Dean, who had been one of the president's most trusted advisors, was jumping ship. Worried about the rapidly deteriorating situation, Dean feared that he was about to be used as a scapegoat to protect the president. Rather than take the fall, Dean began cooperating with federal prosecutors, telling what he knew in hopes that he could avoid a prison sentence.

During the week of April 27, 1973, information from Dean's secret testimony was leaked to the press. The *Washington Post* reported that Dean had given prosecutors detailed information about the roles of John Ehrlichman and H. R. Haldeman in the cover-up scheme. The stories were devastating to Nixon, for the two men were his closest aides and he had come to rely on them for advice.

As public outcry and political pressure mounted, President Nixon was forced to fire both Ehrlichman and Haldeman. When Nixon at last met with them to ask for their resignations, he was despondent. He told his longtime associates that the night before when he went to bed, he hoped "and almost prayed, that I wouldn't wake up in the morning." The true extent of the Watergate scandal was finally sinking in for the president.

The Senate Hearings

On May 17, 1973, Senate hearings into the Watergate scandal officially opened. By now, the scandal had captured the attention of the

The Senate Watergate Committee, chaired by Sam Ervin, began its investigation of the scandal in May 1973. The room was packed with the media and the public, and the hearings were televised, becoming compulsory viewing for the American public as one sordid revelation followed another.

"The burglers who broke into the Democratic National Committee were in effect breaking into the home of every American."

Senator Sam Ervin

> *"There can be no whitewash at the White House."*
>
> Richard Nixon, 1973

entire nation, and the room where the hearings were held was filled to capacity with reporters, television cameras, and curious members of the public. The senator in charge of the hearings was Sam Ervin, a seventy-six-year-old southerner who was prone to quoting both the Bible and the Constitution. He described the gravity of the situation, declaring that the allegations, if proven to be true, threatened "the continued existence of this nation as a representative democracy."

Throughout the summer of 1973, Americans sat glued to their television sets, watching the Senate hearings as if they were an especially gripping soap opera. One of the first witnesses to testify, Watergate burglar James McCord, told of events that sounded like something from a spy thriller. He described a phone call he received from an unknown person, who instructed him to plead guilty and not to accept immunity in exchange for his testimony. He was also told that "the president himself" was aware of the proposed arrangement. As damaging testimony from various witnesses mounted, critics began calling for Nixon's resignation. In his defense, Nixon said that he accepted responsibility for Watergate as "the man at the top," but he insisted that he did not know of the cover-up plans.

But Nixon's denials were soon refuted when John Dean began his testimony. Dean was the first White House insider to come forward, and what he had to say shocked the nation. For hour after hour, in a calm, subdued voice, Dean described a deliberate campaign of political sabotage and the efforts made by Nixon and his aides to conceal the White House connection to Watergate. But

more importantly, Dean answered the crucial question on everyone's mind, "What did the president know and when did he know it?" According to Dean, the president knew plenty, and he had known it for a long time.

At first, Nixon believed he could refute some of Dean's testimony, that it was Dean's word against the president's. But then yet another bomb dropped. This time it came from Alexander Butterfield, a former aide to H. R. Haldeman. During his testimony to the Senate Watergate committee, Butterfield made the shocking revelation that Nixon had a voice-activated taping system in his offices, and that since the spring of 1970, Nixon had been secretly taping private conversations for "historical purposes." The next step was obvious. Everyone investigating the Watergate affair demanded to hear the president's private tapes.

On Top of Everything, the Spiro Agnew Scandal

Just as Nixon was grappling with how to handle the secret tapes, his administration was hit with a new scandal. On August 6, 1973, Vice President Spiro Agnew announced that he was under investigation for allegedly taking kickbacks from contractors, architects, and engineers while governor of Maryland. The payments allegedly continued while Agnew was vice president. Agnew denounced the charges as "false, scurrilous, and malicious," and pledged that he had no intention of resigning. In typical fashion, he lashed out at the press and the Justice Department for being out to "destroy me politically." But as the evidence piled up against

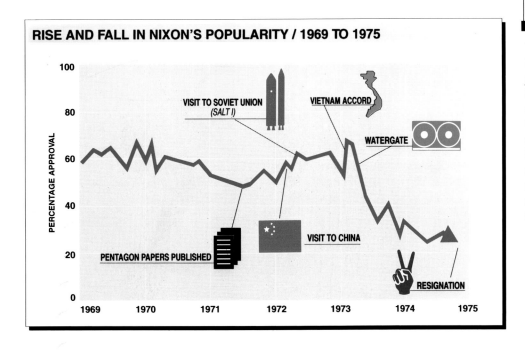

RISE AND FALL IN NIXON'S POPULARITY / 1969 TO 1975

VISIT TO SOVIET UNION
(SALT I)

VIETNAM ACCORD

WATERGATE

PERCENTAGE APPROVAL

VISIT TO CHINA

PENTAGON PAPERS PUBLISHED

RESIGNATION

1969   1970   1971   1972   1973   1974   1975

This chart shows how President Nixon's popularity was boosted by his diplomatic initiatives with China and the Soviet Union, and by the ending of the Vietnam War. The breaking of the Watergate scandal caused a dramatic drop in his popularity, which continued to fall until he resigned from office.

him, Agnew began changing his tone.

On October 10, Agnew pleaded no contest to charges of tax evasion, which the judge said was the equivalent of an admission of guilt. As part of a bargain with the Justice Department, all other charges were dropped, and Agnew resigned from office. The news astonished an already befuddled public. After Spiro Agnew's resignation, Nixon nominated Republican Congressman Gerald Ford to fill the vacancy. On December 6, he was confirmed by the Senate.

The Battle Over the Tapes

While Agnew was battling the Justice Department, Nixon was being drawn into confrontations over his secret recordings. Not only was the Senate committee attempting to procure tapes of White House conversations, but so was the Watergate

special prosecutor, Archibald Cox. When Cox was appointed special prosecutor, he had been promised complete freedom to conduct an independent investigation of the Watergate scandal without any interference. Now both Cox and the Senate committee confronted a major obstacle — the president of the United States. Nixon refused to hand over the tapes, claiming "executive privilege." He said that giving in to the demands to disclose private White House conversations would compromise the posture of the presidency and set a bad precedent.

Cox was not satisfied with that answer and subpoenaed nine White House tapes. The courts decided in favor of Cox and ruled that the president should surrender the tapes. Nixon, still seeking a way out, proposed a compromise: Under the supervision of a Democratic senator, Nixon would prepare a summary of the contents of the tapes to turn over to the courts, and in return, Cox

The Committee to Impeach the President demonstrates outside the White House in October 1973. Nixon's refusal to hand over his secret tapes and his firing of officials who tried to force him to do so outraged millions of Americans.

"There are only so many lies you can take, and now there has been one too many. Nixon should get his ass out of the White House today."

Senator
Barry Goldwater, 1974

would agree not to seek any more tapes. Cox refused. As special prosecutor, he was still determined to conduct an independent investigation of the Watergate scandal.

Nixon was outraged and ordered that Cox be fired. Rather than carry out those orders, Attorney General Elliot Richardson resigned, as did his Deputy Attorney General William Ruckelshaus when faced with the same choice. The job was left to Solicitor General Robert Bork, who accepted the post of acting attorney general. When the White House announced the firing of Cox and the resignations of Richardson and Ruckelshaus, a huge public outcry arose over the so-called Saturday Night Massacre. The public vented its rage on Washington, and congressional offices were deluged with phone calls, letters, and telegrams demanding that Nixon be impeached.

Once again, Nixon had misjudged the public's perception of the Watergate scandal. Shocked by the furious response to Cox's firing, Nixon backed down. His lawyer announced that the president would turn over the subpoenaed tapes, and Nixon appointed a new special prosecutor, Leon Jaworski.

Shocking Transcripts

Shortly after the Saturday Night Massacre, the House Judiciary Committee opened an inquiry into whether the president should be impeached. In April of 1974, the committee subpoenaed the tapes of more than forty conversations. With his back against the wall, Nixon made a surprising decision. He announced that he would turn over transcripts of the tapes. The next day, a 1,308-page volume of transcripts was not only sent to the committee but released to the public as well.

Throughout the transcripts, portions deemed "unrelated to presidential actions" were deleted, but what remained was plenty shocking. Americans who rushed out to buy the transcripts were appalled at the rough conversations that took place between Nixon and his top aides. The phrase "expletive deleted" was used to replace vulgar language so frequently that it became the subject of many jokes.

But the revelations in the transcripts were no laughing matter. The transcripts showed that Dean met with Nixon on March 21, 1973, to discuss problems that were developing with the "hush money" scheme. Dean explained that Howard Hunt was blackmailing the White House, demanding more money to keep quiet. The president asked how much

transcripts: "It is fascinating and depressing, but more depressing than fascinating. And in that it's a good symbol of the Watergate mess."

The Final Fall

While the public reeled over all the transcripts, Special Prosecutor Jaworski was trying to get sixty-four more tapes from the president. He took his case to the Supreme Court,

WATERGATE

For further information see primary source entries on pages

12: 1673-80

President Nixon agreed to turn over the transcripts of over forty conversations. He said, "I realize these transcripts will provide grist for many sensational stories in the press." This turned out to be an understatement. The public bought the transcripts and read them avidly.

money would be needed to keep the Watergate defendants quiet. "I would say these people are going to cost a million dollars over the next two years," said Dean. "We could get that. . . . You could get it in cash," said Nixon. "I know where it could be gotten."

The news commentator John Chancellor summed up how most American people felt after reading the

and on July 24, 1974, the Court ruled against the president. One of the tapes that Nixon was now required to surrender covered the crucial conversation in which Haldeman and Nixon discussed using the CIA to stop the FBI investigation of Watergate. Nixon's closest advisors, after listening to the tape, told Nixon that this was the "smoking gun" investigators had been looking for — clear evidence

Nixon gives the double victory sign as he boards a helicopter to take him back to California after resigning the presidency. A month later, President Ford pardoned Nixon. It was an unpopular move that convinced many people that the government still could not be trusted.

that the president had been involved in the obstruction of justice. Meanwhile, the House Judiciary Committee had voted for three articles, or charges, of impeachment: obstructing justice by covering up the White House role in the Watergate break-in, abusing power by harassing critics through government agencies, and defying committee subpoenas to turn over the tapes.

Obviously the end was near for Nixon. The only question that remained was whether he would resign or stay and fight to the finish, as some of his advisors and family members recommended. After days of wavering back and forth, the president finally made his decision.

On August 8, 1974, Richard Nixon appeared on television to announce that, effective at noon the next day, he was resigning from the presidency. In explaining his reasoning, he said:

I have never been a quitter. To leave office before my term is completed is opposed to every instinct in my body. But as president I must put the interests of America first. To continue to fight through the months ahead for my personal vindication would almost totally absorb the time and attention of both the president and the Congress.

In the months and years that followed Nixon's resignation over the Watergate scandal, political critics and average Americans alike tried to answer the burning question — How did this happen? How did a law-and-order president end up falling from power after trying to skirt the law? Some say that because of Nixon's controlling personality, he thought he could maneuver his way out of Watergate just as he had skillfully managed other crises he faced. Others point out that Nixon was a loner who trusted very few people. Even before Watergate, people talked about the "Berlin Wall" that Haldeman and Ehrlichman had built around the president. He was also said to be very vindictive toward people he regarded as enemies. Perhaps all of these personality traits combined to cause the downfall of Richard Nixon.

President Ford and the Aftermath

The man who became the thirty-eighth president of the United States

had never sought that position. Elected to government only by the constituents of his former Michigan congressional district, Gerald Ford was now the leader of the nation. He inherited a chaotic legacy: the spread of communism in Southeast Asia, an energy crisis, rapid inflation, and, worst of all, a deeply distrustful public. The bloody battles of Watergate had all but shattered the American people's faith in their government.

Though he lacked charisma, Ford seemed to be just the president the nation needed after Watergate. His reputation as a hard-working, trustworthy politician was a welcome change after the devious, vengeful image that Nixon had projected. Many people viewed Ford as a fresh start for the country. In the first month of his presidency, Gerald Ford enjoyed tremendous popularity. He chose Nelson Rockefeller, one of the wealthiest men in the U.S. and a progressive Republican, as his vice president. This move upset party stalwarts but proved Ford's independence. And, by announcing a limited amnesty for draft dodgers and military deserters of the Vietnam War, Ford proved his intentions to begin the healing.

But less than one month after being sworn in, Ford took a step that caused his popularity to plunge. On September 8, President Ford pardoned Nixon for any crimes or offenses he may have committed while president. Ford later said that he pardoned Nixon because he feared a lengthy trial would further divide the nation. But a great many Americans were still bitter over Watergate and wanted to see Nixon punished. Rumors spread that a deal had been arranged: the presidency in exchange for a pardon. Though Ford

testified before Congress to dispel those rumors, to many people, Ford's pardon was proof that government still couldn't be trusted.

The CIA and the FBI Exposed

As if Watergate weren't enough to shake Americans' faith in their government, the public was also given reason to distrust, and even fear, two secretive governmental agencies: the Central Intelligence Agency and the Federal Bureau of Investigation. In the early seventies, a wave of investigative reporting exposed illegal and unconstitutional behavior by both the CIA and FBI. In response, both houses of Congress set up investigative committees to examine the U.S. intelligence establishment.

Americans soon learned that not only had the CIA engaged in illegal spying on domestic dissidents, it had also been involved in assassination attempts against foreign leaders, including Cuban President Fidel Castro. In 1974, Ford confirmed suspicions that the CIA had been involved in the overthrow of Chile's Marxist President Allende in 1973. Allende was killed in the coup and replaced by General Pinochet (backed by the United States), whose regime then committed extensive human rights violations.

It was revealed that the FBI had conducted many operations that violated the constitutional rights of U.S. citizens. In the late sixties and early seventies, the FBI conducted illegal experiments with drugs, tried to sabotage radical groups, and wiretapped and bugged the phones and hotel rooms of Martin Luther King, Jr. These operations had all been

> *"As we bind up the internal wounds of Watergate, more painful and poisonous than those of foreign wars, let us restore the Golden Rule to our political process. And let brotherly love purge our hearts of suspicion and of hate."*
>
> President Gerald Ford, in his inaugural address

Gerald Ford had replaced Spiro Agnew as vice president in late 1973. Less than a year later, he found himself president, trying to restore the people's faith in their government.

conducted while the FBI was led by J. Edgar Hoover, its long-time head, who had built the FBI into a powerful agency. Hoover's battles against gangsters in the thirties and his efforts to root out spies during World War II earned him a reputation as a patriot and a tough crime fighter. But in the sixties, Hoover's anticommunist crusade led him to suspect all antiwar protesters, civil rights activists, in short, all dissidents, as threats to national security. When Hoover died in 1972, President Nixon and other conservatives eulogized him as a great American, but just before his death, a Harris Poll revealed that the public was split in its opinion of Hoover. In the following years, as evidence of Hoover's paranoid plots were revealed, his reputation sank further.

Coming on top of the Vietnam War and Watergate, the exposure of CIA and FBI abuses only endorsed an already growing public distrust. It's no wonder then that, when polled for a 1975 national opinion survey, 69 percent of the respondents agreed that "over the last ten years, this country's leaders have consistently lied to the people."

CHAPTER 5
The Struggle for Social Equality

Following Up What the Sixties Started

After the upheaval of the tumultuous sixties, the old social order in the United States suddenly didn't seem so impervious to change anymore. The civil rights movement, antiwar demonstrations, and student rebellions all proved that when people organized to challenge the established order with determination and solidarity, they could create change. And those changes didn't end with the sixties.

After the dramatic victories of the civil rights movement, in the sixties African-Americans were finally exercising the power of the ballot, but it still remained to be seen what changes that power would bring. And, though the valiant efforts of civil rights activists brought about the end to government-enforced segregation in the South, it also still remained to be seen if the same tactics would work in the North, where discrimination and prejudice were in many ways harder to root out and confront.

As African-Americans strove to achieve equal rights, the quest also spread to other segments of the population. Many women, ethnic minorities, and gays were no longer content to accept a lesser role in society. Instead of losing their ethnic identity to become part of the "melting pot," Latinos, American Indians, and other minorities began celebrating their ethnic heritage.

For people who had long felt excluded from the power structure in the U.S., it was exhilarating to feel that they were finally being heard. But even as the cry for equal rights grew louder, some people began to wonder how these changes would affect society. Some Americans feared that their country was becoming more and more fragmented, with the focus on "us" against "them."

The New Immigrants

Coinciding with the increase in ethnic pride was an increase in the number of immigrants arriving in the U.S., especially from Asian and Latin American countries. In 1965, President Johnson signed a new immigration law designed to reform an earlier policy that favored western European immigrants while discriminating against Asians and others. As a result of the new law, the seventies saw a sharp rise in immigrants arriving from Costa Rica, Jamaica, Nigeria, India, Korea, the Philippines, and other countries that had not been traditional sources of immigrants. Having seen depictions of U.S. affluence on American television shows, many left their Third World homelands in search of a better standard of living. Others came as refugees fleeing persecution in countries including

> **IMMIGRATION**
>
> For further information see primary source entries on pages
>
> **11:** 1454-60, 1484-85, 1490-91, 1514-16;
> **12:** 1696-98, 1715-17

Vietnam and Haiti. The new immigrants settled into established ethnic neighborhoods or created new ones in large cities across the country.

The Women's Movement Picks Up Speed

After the first feminist movement in the early decades of the twentieth century achieved the long-sought goal of suffrage with the Nineteenth Amendment in 1920, it lost momentum and faded from the news. But amid the climate of social change in the late sixties, the second wave of feminism began to build. At first, the revived women's movement was considered too radical by many mainstream men and women alike, but in the seventies, the movement gained the momentum of a grassroots crusade.

One of the women's movement's most basic goals was an end to job discrimination. As more and more women entered the job market (by 1975, women made up almost 40 percent of the workforce), they ran headlong into gender-based barriers. The classified ads of most newspapers were still divided into two sections in the early seventies: "Help Wanted — Male" and "Help Wanted —

Jesse Jackson.

Described by some as "the man who would be king," Jesse Jackson was expected by many, including perhaps himself, to become the new leader of the civil rights movement after the death of Martin Luther King, Jr.

In 1971, Jackson left the Southern Christian Leadership Conference (SCLC), which King led, to begin his own organization, Operation PUSH (People United to Save Humanity). As the leader of PUSH, Jackson's seemingly boundless energy and flashy speaking style kept him in the public eye. By coming up with rhyming phrases such as "Don't put dope in your veins, put hope in your brains," Jackson was sure to be quoted.

In the seventies, Jackson acknowledged a change in goals for the black movement: "The issue is no longer moving in where we were once locked out," he said. "The issue now is moving up." Specifically, his goal was economic self-dependence for African-American communities. Jackson organized boycotts against businesses that exploited blacks and began an annual showcase for African-American businesses called Black Expo.

In the mid-1970s, with PUSH in debt, Jackson began focusing his attention on a more basic problem: the despair of inner-city blacks that was leading to high rates of school dropouts, crime, drug abuse, alcoholism, and teenaged parenthood. In 1977, he began a program called PUSH Excel (PUSH for Excellence). The goal of the program was to teach self-discipline and self-reliance in the schools. Jackson traveled around the country, giving inspirational speeches and calling on students to join him in his rallying cry, "I am somebody!"

The press gave PUSH Excel favorable attention and the program quickly raised huge sums of money, but it was not immune to criticism. One complaint was that the program was too vague. Columnist Clarence Page pointed out that "almost no one can explain what PUSH Excel really is." Others accused Jackson of starting the program to bail PUSH out of its financial crisis. Still others said Jackson was blaming the victim by claiming that all that was holding back African-Americans was their lack of self-discipline. To that criticism, Jackson responded, "The victim is not responsible for being down, but he is responsible for getting up."

César Chávez. (1927-1993)

In the mid-sixties, César Chávez gained worldwide attention and some would even say hero status for his efforts to organize migrant farm workers in California. Through Chávez's tireless determination, the migrant workers, long ignored and exploited, began to receive higher wages, health insurance, and other benefits they had been denied. A small, quiet man, Chávez devoted his life to La Causa, as he called the movement. Following the example of Gandhi, he used nonviolent methods to achieve his goals, including strikes, boycotts, marches, and fasting.

When Chávez called on consumers to boycott grapes in order to pressure growers to honor his farm workers union, an estimated seventeen million Americans stopped buying grapes. After five years, the strike and boycott forced growers to sign the union contracts in 1970. The triumph was hailed as a David over Goliath victory, and by 1972, Chávez had sixty thousand workers under contract with his union.

The contracts expired in 1973, however, and the growers, who were wary of Chávez's "radical" union, sought to weaken his power by inviting in the more acceptable International Brotherhood of Teamsters. A feud between the two unions ensued as the Teamsters managed to steal away a large number of UFW contracts. Chávez accused the Teamsters of signing "sweetheart deals" with the growers and called another strike. The strike ended, however, when one of the union members was shot and killed on the picket line.

In 1975, California Governor Jerry Brown, a supporter of Chávez, signed into law the Agricultural Labor Relations Act, which established collective bargaining for farm workers and provided for secret ballot elections, making it impossible for the Teamsters to steal away contracts. Though the law represented a victory for Chávez, his movement seemed to be losing momentum. His earlier tactics, which had been so effective and gained him widespread support, were losing their impact, and critics charged that he was unable to evolve his organization from a social movement to an effective union. Growers accused him of mismanaging the union, and several of Chávez's aides quit in frustration. Despite the criticism, Chávez continued his battle, and to many people, he remained a heroic figure until his death in 1993.

Female." The vast majority of the "female" jobs involved clerical, domestic, or other relatively low-paying work. In 1974, a comparison of median incomes for men and women revealed that men made 75 percent more than women. Even women with four years of college earned less than men who had not gone past eighth grade.

Another goal was to put an end to the unwritten rule that gave women the primary responsibility for housework and child care. Both employed women and full-time homemakers were seeking a more just division of labor at home.

Changing Attitudes

Feminists believed that before equal rights could truly be achieved, society would have to change its perception of women, and women would have to change their view of themselves. But the problem was how to alter the deeply embedded attitudes that confined and limited the role of women in society.

One attempted solution to the problem was consciousness-raising groups, small gatherings of women who met regularly to give each other the courage and support they needed

"If women had wives to keep house for them, to stay home with vomiting children, to get the car fixed, fight with the painters, run to the supermarket, reconcile the bank statements, listen to everyone's problems, cater the dinner parties, and nourish the spirit each night, just imagine the possibilities for expansion — the number of books that would be written, companies started, professorships filled, political offices that would be held, by women."

Gail Sheehy, *Passages*, 1976

to try to change their roles. In an article entitled "The Housewife's Moment of Truth," Jane O'Reilly wrote about the moment when women experienced the "click" of recognition that they did not have to play the old role. "In Houston, Texas," she wrote, "a friend of mine stood and watched her husband step over a pile of toys on the stairs, put there to be carried up. 'Why can't you get this stuff put away?' he mumbled. Click! 'You have two hands,' she said, turning away."

As another step toward changing attitudes, the women's movement sought to promote gender-free language. For example, the terms "spokesperson" and "chairperson" came into use instead of "spokesman" and "chairman" to reinforce the idea that one didn't have to be a man to fill those positions. By the end of the decade, the term "Ms." had gained acceptance as an alternative to "Mrs." or "Miss," which, as feminist Gloria Steinem said, "removed the necessity

of identifying all females by the presence or absence of a man."

In January of 1972, Steinem and several other feminists launched a magazine called *Ms.* Controlled and operated entirely by women, *Ms* provided a forum for feminists and offered an alternative to the traditional women's magazines such as *Ladies Home Journal.* Its editors also vowed not to include any advertising they deemed sexist.

The Fight for ERA

In addition to fighting for equal rights on the home front, at work, and through language, the women's movement also sought to put an end to institutionalized discrimination against women. Groups such as the National Organization for Women (NOW) worked to guarantee women equal rights through legislation, often with great success. But one of the most important goals of the women's

Feminists march in celebration of the fifty-first anniversary of women's suffrage in 1971, chanting "We want 51 percent of everything."

Thousands march in support of the Equal Rights Amendment in Springfield, Illinois, in 1976. The amendment failed because conservative religious and political groups organized to fight it using scary, false scenarios of what passage would mean in people's lives such as the drafting of women in case of war.

"*Eliminating the patriarchal and racist base of the existing social system requires a revolution, not a reform.*"

First issue of
Ms magazine

movement remained elusive — a constitutional amendment to prohibit discrimination on the basis of sex.

The Equal Rights Amendment was originally proposed in 1923, during the first wave of feminism. When the fight for the ERA was revived in the late sixties, its chances for passing appeared very good, as polls indicated that a majority of Americans agreed women needed a guarantee of equal rights. In 1972, the ERA passed in Congress by an overwhelming margin. Feminists were ecstatic, but the fight was not over yet. The amendment needed to be ratified by three-fourths of the states by March 22, 1979 — the deadline imposed by Congress.

At first, the deadline seemed to pose no problem, for by the end of 1972, twenty-two states had already ratified. But overconfident supporters of the ERA underestimated the task ahead of them: Though they needed thirty-eight states to pass the amendment, their opponents needed to block ratification in only thirteen states to defeat the ERA.

Backlash and the Anti-ERA Campaign

Opposition to the ERA came mainly from conservative religious and political organizations, including the John Birch Society, the Mormons, and George Wallace's American Party. By 1974, they had a well-organized anti-ERA campaign underway. One of the most effective enemies of the ERA was Phyllis Schlafly, a conservative political activist who organized a group called Stop ERA. She declared:

The claim that American women are downtrodden and unfairly treated is the fraud of the century. The truth is that American women have never had it so good. Why should we lower ourselves to "equal rights" when we already have the status of special privilege?

The anti-ERA groups painted a frightening picture of what the ERA would lead to. Yet the proposed amendment declared simply: "Equality of rights under the law shall not be denied or abridged by the United States or by any state on account of sex." Opponents of the

A view of the National Women's Conference in Houston, Texas, 1977. Women hoped to develop a National Plan of Action, but its more radical elements proved controversial.

amendment turned that statement around to claim that the ERA would mean mothers could be forced into combat duty and that they would be denied alimony and child support. Others called the proposed amendment a "socialistic plan to destroy the home." When pro-ERA groups failed to refute the opposition quick-

1977. For women all over the country, the huge gathering was a source of great pride, but the purpose of the conference, to develop a National Plan of Action, brought out divisions within the movement and led to controversy. Among the myriad of issues addressed in the plan were child care, media representation of

ly and convincingly, a sense of confusion began to surround the ERA. Humorist Erma Bombeck said of the amendment, "Twenty-four words have never been so misunderstood since the four words, 'One size fits all.'"

The growing confusion and mixed feelings surrounding the ERA and the women's movement in general were evident during the National Women's Conference held in Houston, Texas, in November of

women, rape, and battered women. But some women walked out of the conference when the plan supported more controversial ideas, including homosexual and lesbian rights as well as guaranteed access to legal abortion for all women. Anti-ERA groups seized on the most controversial elements of the plan as evidence that feminist supporters of the ERA had a radical agenda.

As the deadline for passage of the ERA drew near, supporters launched

Conservative activist Phyllis Schlafly speaks, also in Houston, at a rally of opponents of the National Women's Conference. In the arena are posters citing Christian ethics and denouncing the ERA, abortion, and lesbian rights.

a public information campaign to counter the misinformation being spread by the opposition, and NOW organized boycotts of states that had not ratified the amendment. But by then, it was too late. Although Congress extended the deadline by three years in 1978, the opposition was now entrenched. Passage of ERA, once considered a sure thing, grew less and less likely.

Abortion: the "Lightning Rod"

Though the fight for the ERA was more difficult than feminists had anticipated, the right to a legal abortion came surprisingly quickly. As the women's movement was growing stronger in the late sixties and early seventies, Americans began taking a

A demonstration to repeal New York's liberal abortion laws takes place in April 1972. A garbage can full of dolls emphasizes the demonstrators' message that, in their view, abortion is murder.

more liberal view of abortion. Feminists argued that women should have ultimate control over their bodies, including the right to end a pregnancy. By 1973, four states agreed, permitting abortion on demand. Efforts were also underway in other states to strike down restrictions on abortion.

Then, with one Supreme Court decision, *Roe v. Wade*, abortion was legalized in every state. In a seven-to-two decision, the Court ruled that a woman's right to privacy made government interference with abortion unconstitutional during the first three months of pregnancy; during the second three months, the state was allowed to regulate abortion to protect the mother's health; and during the last trimester, the state could bar abortion.

Though the decision was hailed as a great victory by the women's movement, it threw much of the nation into a state of moral turmoil. Heated debates over at what point life begins and whether the mother's right to privacy supersedes the fetus's right to life did not end with the Supreme Court decision. Catholics and members of the Right to Life movement, which had been gathering steam before the decision, were stunned and outraged by the development.

Time magazine pointed out that a Gallup Poll conducted shortly before the Supreme Court ruling showed that 46 percent of Americans favored a woman's right to choose an abortion without government interference during the first trimester, and 45 percent opposed the idea. As the article accurately predicted, "Such a close division of sentiment can only ensure that while the matter has been settled legally, it remains a lightning rod for intense national debate." For the rest of the decade and beyond, the issue of abortion continued to divide Americans.

The Struggle for Equality Continues

As the title of a book compiled by the editors of *Ms* magazine declares, the seventies truly was *The Decade of Women*. In almost every area — business, politics, medicine, sports — women made important inroads. Between 1972 and 1983, the proportion of women in state legislatures tripled, and in 1979, there were more women than men in colleges and universities for the first time in U.S. history.

But at the end of the decade, women still faced plenty of obstacles to equality. Cooking, cleaning, and child care were still considered "women's work" by most men, and the economic gap between the sexes was still formidable.

One of the most difficult problems facing women was the growing feminization of poverty. Between 1964 and 1974, the divorce rate in the U.S. doubled, and a greater number of women than ever before were trying to make it on their own. Divorced women and unwed mothers entering the job market were faced with the fact that women earned on average just over half of what men made, and with child care difficult to find, many women did not have the option to work. On top of it all, the economy was stuck in a recession, making jobs hard to come by for everyone. All of these factors combined to force more and more women into poverty.

WOMEN'S RIGHTS

For further information see primary source entries on pages

11: 1480, 1508-09, 1521-22; **12:** 1713-14, 1717-19

Bella Abzug. (1920-1998)

By the time she was elected to the U.S. House of Representatives from New York in 1970, Bella Abzug already had a reputation as a strong-willed, uncompromising, liberal activist. Beginning in the sixties, Abzug became known as an outspoken critic of the war and an ardent supporter of women's rights. When her constituents sent her to Washington, she was not at all daunted by the nation's capital. On her first day in office, she proposed a bill demanding the withdrawal of all U.S. troops from Vietnam by the Fourth of July, 1971. Though the proposal was shelved, Abzug had announced her presence.

With her trademark broad-brimmed hats, her loud New York accent, and her sometimes strident demeanor, Abzug was a controversial figure. Critics referred to her as "Bellacose Abzug" and "Battling Bella." Abzug worked tirelessly to promote the interests of women, the poor, and minorities, unafraid to challenge the powers in Washington. In 1971, she sponsored a $5 billion child-care bill, which was vetoed by Nixon. She also fought for a women's credit rights bill, equalization of pay between the sexes, and welfare reform.

In 1976, Abzug gave up her seat in the House to run for the Senate but lost the Democratic nomination by less than 1 percent to Daniel Patrick Moynihan. The next year, she made a run for mayor of New York City and lost that race as well. But to those who were predicting an end to her political career she said, "I'll thank you not to write my obituary."

Abzug returned to Washington when President Jimmy Carter named her as co-chair of the National Advisory Committee for Women. Relations between Carter and the committee, especially Abzug, were strained, and when members of the committee criticized the president's budget cutbacks as being especially hard on women, Carter fired Abzug. Over half of the committee resigned in protest.

Abzug entered private legal practice but remained active in women's rights and continued to serve on many government boards, including the Women's Foreign Policy Council. She also published the Guide to Political Power for American Women. In later years, she became increasingly involved in environmental causes.

Beyond the Civil Rights Movement

For African-Americans, too, the seventies was a decade of both great achievements and continuing frustrations. Many of the achievements came through the ballot box. In 1971, thirteen African-American members of the U.S. House of Representatives formed the Congressional Black Caucus to represent the needs of African-Americans. The next year, they were joined by sixteen newly elected black members of Congress, an unprecedented number. Several major cities, including Los Angeles, Detroit, and Atlanta, elected their first African-

Shirley Chisholm.

When Shirley Chisholm was elected to the U.S. House of Representatives from New York in 1968, she became the first African-American woman to hold that position. But Chisholm's ambitions were not satisfied. In 1972, she announced, "I am a candidate for the presidency of the United States. I make that statement proudly, in the full knowledge that, as a black person and as a female person, I do not have a chance of actually gaining that office in this election year. I make that statement seriously, knowing that my candidacy itself can change the face and future of American politics — that it will be important to the needs and hopes of every one of you — even though, in the conventional sense, I will not win."

Indeed, Chisholm did not win in the conventional sense. Leading feminists and the Congressional Black Caucus withheld their endorsements from Chisholm, choosing instead to get behind the more promising Democratic candidate, George McGovern. But still, Chisholm's campaign was an important symbol of future possibilities. She compared her role to the 1928 Catholic candidate for president, Al Smith, who some believe paved the way for the election of John F. Kennedy.

After her presidential campaign, Chisholm returned to the House of Representatives, where she gradually gained power with seniority. In 1977, she gained a position on the influential House Rules Committee. "I have learned through life's best teacher, experience, how to seize power and exercise it," said Chisholm. "In Washington above all places power is what counts. Nothing else matters. Real power is never given, it must be taken."

Chisholm used that power to work for education, women's rights, the poor, and to win grants for black businesses in her struggling district. Though she often spoke out against the "inherent racism" in the United States, she also believed that action was more important than words. "Rhetoric sounds good in the street," she said, "but green in the pocket puts food on the table, clothes on our children, and pride in our men."

American mayors. Among other "firsts" in the seventies were the first black general in the Marine Corps, the first black astronauts, and the first black major league baseball manager.

But even as some race-based barriers were breaking down, other formidable hurdles remained, namely poverty and segregation. The crippling recession of the seventies destroyed many black-owned businesses. Rising crime rates and the sixties' street riots had contributed to "white flight" from the cities, and middle-class blacks also began moving to the suburbs. Too many of those left behind were plagued by poverty, drug abuse, and a rising wave of black-on-black crime.

The Battle Over Busing

By 1970, the 1954 Supreme Court decision forbidding state-sponsored segregation in public schools was finally being enforced in the South. But in the North and West, half of all black students still attended schools that were at least 95 percent black. The reason for this "de facto" (meaning actual although not established by law) segregation was that the schools reflected the surrounding, racially separated neighborhoods. In an attempt to integrate the schools, some cities adopted busing programs that sent students from

"Women in this country must become revolutionaries. We must refuse to accept the old, the traditional roles and stereotypes.... We must replace the old, negative thoughts about our femininity with positive thoughts and positive action."

Shirley Chisholm

Parents protest the busing of their children in Pontiac, Michigan, in 1971. Busing was an important issue in the 1972 presidential campaign, and later protests became violent.

white school districts to predominantly black schools and vice versa. The programs were instantly controversial, but in 1971, the Supreme Court upheld busing as a viable method for desegregating schools.

Busing became a hot issue in the 1972 presidential campaign. Both conservative Nixon and George Wallace sensed a feeling among an increasingly conservative white public that the country had gone far enough to promote racial equality. Pat Buchanan, a Nixon speechwriter and future presidential candidate, advised the president that, "The national mood among blacks and whites alike is toward black separatism and white separatism." George Wallace was running a fairly successful campaign, based, in part, on an antibusing message, before he was paralyzed in an assassination attempt by a disturbed young white man.

Arguments against busing ranged from the blatantly racist to the apparently reasonable. Parents argued that their children would be deprived of a high quality education and worried about them being sent into dangerous black neighborhoods. Both blacks and whites worried that busing would destroy the concept of community schools.

The fight against busing turned violent in Boston when a court-ordered program was set to take place in 1974. South Boston, a largely Irish, working-class community, was affected by the busing plan and residents were deeply resentful of outside intervention in their schools. Violence erupted in the schools and on the streets. Buses carrying black students to previously all-white schools were escorted by police after being pelted with rocks by angry protesters, and an African-American motorist was pulled from his car and nearly killed by a violent mob. President Ford turned down a request for federal troops to quell the violence and was accused of encouraging the unrest when he told reporters, "I have consistently opposed forced busing to achieve racial balance as a solution to quality education and, therefore, I respectfully disagree with the judge's order." In the fall of 1975, over eighteen hundred police, marshals, and National Guardsmen were called on to ensure that the new school year would begin without violence. Many white parents boycotted the schools by keeping their children home. The defiant Boston School Committee vowed to fight the busing ordinance all the way to the Supreme Court, but the Court refused to reopen the case.

Confusion over the issue was exacerbated by a Supreme Court ruling in 1974 that suburban school districts could not be forced to bus their students into Detroit to integrate schools there. By the end of the seventies, busing was curbed in response to public protest, and the controversy subsided. The problem of segregated schools was far from resolved, however. In fact, the situation continued to worsen, as more and more mem-

bers of the white middle class were moving out to the suburbs. As a result, their property taxes were used to fund suburban schools instead of inner city schools. For African-American students in the inner city, schools thus remained underfunded and "separate and unequal."

Affirmative Action

Another controversial policy in the seventies was affirmative action. In an effort to overcome the effects of past discrimination, organizations such as universities, fire departments, and large companies began making an effort to fill positions with a larger proportion of African-Americans. When a white man named Allan Bakke applied to medical school and was turned down as a result of an affirmative action program, he sued the school. The case went before the Supreme Court and, in 1978, the Court handed down what many people felt was an unclear decision. The

A demonstration in San Francisco about the Allan Bakke case in 1978. The Supreme Court did not clarify how affirmative action should be put into practice, although it ruled in favor of Bakke. A year later, the court ruled that private businesses could apply their own affirmative action programs when hiring workers. Many conservatives accused the Supreme Court of sanctioning reverse discrimination.

Court ruled that although race could be one factor involved in the consideration of candidates, strict quotas were prohibited.

The refusal of the Court to provide clear guidelines on affirmative action revealed the confusing phase that the struggle for racial equality had entered in the seventies. In the fifties and sixties, the fight had been against "de jure" (legally based) inequality, and the goals were clear — to reverse the laws that discriminated against blacks. In the seventies, the focus was on "de facto" discrimination, the inequality that, though not enforced by law, nevertheless was a fact of life for most African-Americans. In this new battle, the front lines were harder to discern.

Oscar Running Bear, a member of the American Indian Movement (AIM), which took over the town of Wounded Knee, South Dakota, in 1973. AIM was protesting the government's treatment of American Indians, and the Senate promised an investigation.

American Indian Activists Organize and Protest

In the early sixties, the civil rights movement inspired many American Indian tribes to join forces in an effort to push the government to address their long-neglected concerns. Though some reform legislation was passed and federal aid to American Indians was expanded, serious problems such as high rates of alcoholism and poverty on reservations persisted. In some tribes, the average life expectancy was only forty-six years. In 1972, a militant group called the American Indian Movement (AIM) took over the

offices of the Bureau of Indian Affairs in Washington, D.C., in an effort to focus the nation's attention on their plight.

Indian activists also organized to protest unjust and broken treaties between the federal government and American Indians. In 1973, three hundred members of AIM took over the small town of Wounded Knee, South Dakota, seizing eleven hostages and barricading themselves in a church. AIM chose Wounded Knee not only because they claimed the land was rightfully theirs, but also because the town was a powerful symbol to Indians, for it was there that over three hundred Sioux Indians were massacred by the American cavalry in 1890. In response to the Wounded Knee occupation, the Senate promised an investigation of government-Indian relations, but conflicts continued. As natural resources dwindled, treaties in which tribes retained their traditional and legal right to hunt and fish their former lands in perpetuity became a source of resentment to non-Indian people, and the treaties were threatened. In other cases, however, the federal government took action to right old wrongs by restoring land to Indians. In 1970, for example, forty-eight thousand acres in New Mexico were returned to the Taos Pueblo Indians.

Another important issue to Indian activists was the right to self-determination. For decades, the goal of federal policy was to turn Indians away from their tribal customs and assimilate them into the mainstream culture. But in 1970, the Nixon administration finally renounced that goal, and in 1976, the Indian Self-Determination Act was passed,

encouraging Indians to take control of their own education. But many tribes complained of inadequate federal funding for education. Faced with these and other persistent problems, American Indians continued their efforts to organize and protest.

The Gay Liberation Movement

In 1969, when police raided a gay bar called the Stonewall in Greenwich Village in New York City, it was not an unusual occurrence. But this time, the patrons of the bar fought back, and this resistance to police harassment marked the beginning of the gay liberation movement. Incorporating many of the same tactics used by the women's movement, homosexuals and lesbians began organizing to demand an end to discrimination and prejudice.

By the mid-1970s, gays had become a political force, especially in New York and San Francisco, which had large gay populations. The movement won its battle to have homosexuality removed from the American Psychiatric Association's list of psychiatric disorders, and civil rights ordinances protecting gays were passed in several cities. In 1978, 250,000 people marched in San Francisco on Gay Pride Day. But the gay liberation movement was not without its violent episodes. In 1978, Harvey Milk, an openly gay San Francisco public official, was assassinated. When the killer received the lightest sentence possible, riots erupted.

As the decade progressed, an anti-gay backlash developed. Singer Anita Bryant, allied with conservative religious groups, began a campaign to

CIVIL RIGHTS

For further information see primary source entries on pages

11: 1582-83; **12:** 1627-32, 1635-38, 1643-50, 1652-55

Gay pride parade, New York City, 1973. The gay liberation movement formed as homosexuals became politically active and started to fight back against harassment and discrimination. They were sometimes successful, but the more homosexuality was accepted with changes in the law, the more conservative religious groups objected.

repeal gay rights ordinances in Florida. Similar efforts were made in other states as well. Though the anti-gay backlash revealed a deeply embedded societal antagonism toward homosexuality, it also galvanized the gay liberation movement. The gay movement would need all the strength it could get, for in the next decade, it would confront a much greater threat — AIDS.

Equality in Education

"If there was one dominant theme underlying education events of the seventies, it was the yearning for equality," said Ben Brodinsky, educational consultant and writer. Like the controversial busing policy, many attempts toward providing equal access to education met with strong opposition. Some attempts also culminated in great successes, though there were still plenty of battles to be fought by the end of the decade.

During the seventies, school financing came under scrutiny as a source of educational inequality. In 1971, the California Supreme Court ruled that a reliance on local property taxes as the primary source of funds "may be depriving children of equal protection under the law," for by such a system, wealthy neighborhoods generate more money for their schools than poor neighborhoods. Equal rights advocates were excited by the ruling, but their hopes were shot down when the Supreme Court ruled on a similar case involving fifteen Mexican-American families in 1973. Though the Court urged states to reform their school financing plans, it denied that state governments were obligated to provide equal financing for all public schools. "The poor people have lost again," said defendant Demetrio Rodriquez in response to the ruling.

The fight for bilingual education was more successful, though the movement was not without its opponents. The plight of non-English-speaking students in public schools was addressed in 1965 by the Bilingual Education Act, but it was not until the seventies that the government began providing federal dollars for bilingual education. Advocates complained that the funds were not enough to meet the needs of the millions of Latinos, Asians, and American Indians in public schools, but some critics were angry that any money was being spent to teach children in their native tongues. They argued that bilingual education discouraged students from assimilating into American culture and was therefore counterproductive, a debate that continues today.

In 1974, the Mexican American Legal Defense and Education Fund (MALDEF), an organization which was fighting to prevent discrimination against Mexican-Americans in employment, politics, and education, won an important case that resulted in a guarantee of bilingual education for non-English-speaking students in public schools. MALDEF's president, Vilma Martinez, gained the ear of important political leaders, including U.S. presidents Ford and Carter.

The struggle for equal access to education was also extended to the disabled as Americans became more sensitive to the obstacles faced by that segment of the population. In 1975, Congress passed the Education for All Handicapped Children Act, which stated that "free, appropriate public

Angela Davis.

In the late sixties, Angela Davis, a Communist, feminist, civil rights activist, and philosophy teacher, became the center of a stormy controversy over academic freedom when she was fired from her position at University of California, Los Angeles. In fact, she became such a controversial figure that, in response to numerous death threats, Davis bought several guns to protect herself.

Then, in 1970, in an attempt to free three African-American prisoners, gunmen raided the Marin County courthouse. The unsuccessful raid left a judge and three others dead. When the guns turned out to be registered in Davis's name, she was charged with kidnapping, conspiracy, and murder. The FBI placed Davis on their ten-most-wanted fugitives list, and the hunt for Davis became a national drama. Two months later, she was arrested in New York.

A "Free Angela" movement quickly developed, and supporters demonstrated outside the prison where she was being held as well as in cities around the world. Communist East Germany made Davis a cause célèbre, turning her into a Marxist martyr. After spending sixteen months in prison, Davis was acquitted of all charges.

Building on the activism surrounding the "Free Angela" movement, Davis founded an organization called the National Alliance against Racist and Political Repression. A prolific writer, she also traveled the world lecturing on women's rights, sexism, racism, political and judicial reform, and the rights of prisoners. Though by the late seventies her huge afro hairdo, once a symbol of Black Pride, had been trimmed to a chic length, Davis still was a member of the Communist party. She was still devoted to the struggle for social equality, but she denounced the use of violence. "Terrorist groups aren't accomplishing anything at all," she said, "because you need the majority of the people to accomplish a revolution."

education" should be available to all disabled children between the ages of three and eighteen. But meeting the needs of disabled students required a massive effort and expensive changes in school facilities. By the end of the decade, "the pain, struggle, and red tape of meeting federal mandates on behalf of the handicapped promoted a rising volume of complaints and doubts among educators," reported Brodinsky.

While the debates over equality in education raged on, Americans were also growing increasingly concerned about the quality of education provided by public schools. In 1975, Americans were shocked to learn that scores on the Scholastic Aptitude

Tests (SATs) had dropped an average of ten points in the verbal section and eight points on the mathematics section in just one year. Other reports indicated that 13 percent of high school graduates were functionally illiterate. In response to such disturbing trends, a "Back-to-Basics" movement took hold in many school districts. Proponents of the movement blamed the sixties emphasis on relevance in the curriculum for taking the focus away from the basic skills and knowledge traditionally taught in schools.

Yet another problem facing education was a sharp decline in enrollment. During 1971 and 1972, school enrollments dropped by a half million students in the United States. Part of the decline was caused by the aging of the baby-boomer generation, but the lower numbers in public schools were also evidence of families who had given up on the system and enrolled their children in private schools. Declining enrollments did not mean lower school budgets, however, for school buildings still needed to be maintained. In fact, the high rate of inflation made it more expensive than ever to run a school. Rising costs and declining test scores made for an unsettling combination, and by the end of the seventies, Americans were seriously questioning the future of their educational system.

Equality and the Death Penalty

Throughout the history of the United States, public opinion on capital punishment has fluctuated. Amid the drive for liberal reforms in the late sixties, the percentage of Americans who approved of the death penalty fell to a new low of only 42 percent. Some argued the death penalty was unconstitutional because it qualified as "cruel and unusual punishment." Others argued that capital punishment was disproportionately imposed on African-Americans and therefore amounted to racial discrimination. In 1967, the U.S. began a moratorium on capital punishment while the Supreme Court examined the issue.

In 1972, the Court ruled that the death penalty was indeed unconstitutional in the manner in which it was being imposed. Justice William O. Douglas noted that it affected the "poor and despised unequally," while Justice Potter Stewart decried the quite arbitrary nature of the death-sentencing process, comparing it to "being struck by lightning." As a result of the ruling, almost six hundred prisoners were released from death row, and their sentences were commuted to life imprisonment.

By the middle of the 1970s, however, public opinion was swinging back in favor of capital punishment, as the conservative backlash described earlier began to permeate the social atmosphere. In 1976, a poll showed that 65 percent of those questioned now favored the death penalty. Reflecting public opinion, thirty-five states revised their capital punishment statutes in an effort to meet the Supreme Court's standards. In 1976, the Court ruled that as long as juries were given a set of factors to consider when sentencing, capital punishment did not violate the Constitution. On January 17, 1977, the moratorium on capital punishment came to an end when convicted murderer Gary Gilmore was killed by a firing squad in Utah.

CHAPTER 6
The "Me Decade"
and Other Social Trends

"The Times They Are A-changing"

Though the radicals of the sixties did not achieve their goal of "Revolution Now!" the youth movement did bring about major changes in American society. Their challenges to social conventions and their focus on individual freedom caused many people to step back and rethink their lives. The upheaval of the sixties continued to reverberate through the seventies as more and more Americans experimented with alternatives to a traditional lifestyle. In the past, loyalty to one's family, God, and country had formed a framework for accepted morals and values. But now the social environment was changing, and there was a growing emphasis on self-fulfillment, or as some put it, on "doing your own thing." The change affected how people played and worshiped, and, most noticeably, it affected the American family.

The Changing Family

In the late sixties and throughout the seventies, the divorce rate rose dramatically in the United States. Social analysts point to a number of factors to explain the alarming increase, including higher personal expectations for marriage and the women's movement, which promoted alternatives to the traditional roles of subservient wife and mother. In addition, the social stigma of divorce was quickly fading, and the passage of no-fault divorce laws made it easier than ever to end a marriage. Perhaps with an eye toward the failure rate of marriages, more and more couples were opting to bypass the institution altogether and live together openly without being married, a lifestyle commonly referred to only a few years earlier as "living in sin."

As marriage changed, so did the family unit. One of the most notable trends was the increase in the number of children born out of wedlock. Between 1960 and 1978, the rate more than tripled, from 5.3 percent

Turning accepted behavior on its head, this scene shows a car decorated as if for a wedding sitting outside a bar while its owners celebrate their divorce. In the 1970s, divorce was on the increase and easy to obtain. At the same time, many people chose not to get married at all, and more younger people decided to live together unwed or remain single for longer.

of all births to 16.3 percent. As for married women, they were having fewer children and waiting longer to have them. In 1967, only 7 percent of women polled by the Census Bureau intended to have just one child or remain childless. By 1975, that number had increased to 17 percent. The reasons for the lower birth rates included more accessible birth control, legalized abortion, the increase in the number of working women, and the poor economy, which made it difficult to support a family.

The changing American family created many ripple effects. For example, between the mid-1960s and the late 1970s, the number of married mothers who worked outside the home nearly doubled, creating a huge demand for child-care services. Though the number of daycare centers and preschools grew quickly in the seventies, the search for quality child care remained a dilemma for many families with employed parents. Another noticeable change was that more and more families were turning to child psychiatrists and family counselors to help them deal with the stress of divorce and other changes affecting the seventies' family.

Not only was the divorce rate rising, but many people were putting off marriage and, as a result, a greater portion of the population than ever before was now living alone. In fact, the number of people under thirty-five living alone more than doubled during the decade. To cater to the rising population of "singles," apartment complexes known as singles communities were developed, and singles bars sprang up across the country. Along the same lines, older Americans were also developing their own communities. In the past, grandma and grandpa often moved in with their children after retiring. But an increasing number of senior citizens were choosing instead to live in retirement villages, where their needs were catered to and where they were surrounded by people with whom they had much in common.

The changing American lifestyle was revealed in not only how people cared for their children and where they chose to live, but also in how they ate. With more wives and mothers working outside the home than ever before, and with the increase in the number of people living alone, many Americans were looking for alternatives to home cooking. By 1977, one in every three dollars spent on food went to restaurants and fast-food emporia.

The "Me Decade"

In the seventies, the baby boomers were given a new name — the "Me Generation." The name came from an essay by writer Tom Wolfe – entitled, "The Me Decade and the Third Great Awakening," in which he theorizes that after three decades of prosperity following World War II, Americans had more time and money than ever before to concentrate on "Me." This focus on the self was especially prevalent among the young and affluent in the seventies. Though in the sixties the youth movement had focused on public concerns and social reforms, there seemed to be a general retreat in the seventies into private, some would even say selfish, concerns. For some, the path to happiness was self-indulgence, while for others it was self-awareness, but it always began with the self.

> "[This is a time of] hedonism ... narcissism ... cult of the self."
>
> Christopher Lasch, *New York Review of Books*

A drug addict melts heroin powder to a liquid so that she can inject it. Drug use was rising, and users had to find a lot of money to keep the habit going. By the late 1970s, cocaine, which gave an instant high and was very expensive, was becoming more popular.

The pursuit of pleasure combined with the sixties rejection of traditional morals led to the so-called sexual revolution. Among certain social circles, the idea of open marriages (where married partners agree to allow sexual relationships outside the marriage) became trendy, and surveys suggested an increase in extramarital affairs. Drug use was also on the rise, as the Me Generation experimented with altered consciousness. Marijuana use, once a symbol of hippie rebellion, grew more widespread in the early seventies. Some even called it a national epidemic. By the late seventies, cocaine use, too, was on the rise. An expensive drug that caused an instant high, cocaine became the ultimate symbol of self-indulgence.

The Search for Self

Some people chose an inner path to self-gratification, looking for spiritual and psychological ways to "get in touch with themselves." Building on the counterculture's search for meaning in the sixties, an ever-increasing number of people were turning to a variety of disciplines in an effort to "find" themselves and "get their heads together." As philosopher Jacob Needleman explained, "From 'getting what you want,' the idea of happiness has been transformed into 'changing who you are.'" The methods ranged from age-old religions to fly-by-night programs promising instant enlightenment — for a price. Not only young adults but homemakers and executives as well began experimenting with everything from primal scream therapy to transcendental meditation to yoga.

The so-called consciousness movement included elements of modern Western psychotherapy as well as disciplines from ancient Eastern religions. One of the most popular paths to self-enlightenment in the seventies was "est," or Erhard Seminars Training. Like many of the new religions and self-improvement programs that grew popular in the seventies, est was centered around a celebrity guru. Werner Erhard, a former used-car salesman and personnel motivator, created a multimillion dollar enterprise by selling enlightenment. Said Erhard at one est seminar:

I am here to explain what can't be explained. The goal of the training is "getting it," but you don't "get it" in the training. You get that you've got it in the training. In the Tao, "it" is the way it is. In Zen, "it" is the suchness. In "est" we call "it" riding the horse in the direction it is going.

So for the price of $250, self-seekers met for two consecutive weekends to undergo intensive est training, which included mind and body exercises aimed at teaching the lesson that "I am the cause of my own world."

One of the exercises involved "attacking the ego" in order to "free" the individual by first telling that person everything that was wrong with him or her. Why would anyone pay to be verbally assaulted? According to Tom Wolfe:

The appeal was simple enough. It is summed up in the notion: "Let's talk about Me." No matter whether you managed to renovate your personality through encounter sessions or not, you had finally focused your attention and your energies on the most fascinating subject on earth: Me.

Wolfe was not the only critic who saw self-centered motives behind the consciousness movement, or, as some preferred to call it, "the new narcissism." Social analysts feared that people were so concerned with improving themselves that they were becoming less socially conscious and politically inactive. But others claimed that after Vietnam and Watergate, people who used to be social activists had given up on improving the big picture and instead were concentrating on improving themselves. They were now striving toward an "inner revolution."

Former radical and Chicago Seven defendant Jerry Rubin seems to be proof of that theory. In his book *Growing (Up) At 37*, the ex-revolutionary writes:

In five years, from 1971 to 1975, I directly experienced est, gestalt therapy, bioenergetics, rolfing, massage, jogging,

Tom Wolfe.

With his year-round white suits, his high starched collars, and his unconventional writing style, Tom Wolfe became one of the most recognizable authors of the seventies. He first emerged in the sixties as a witty writer who vividly captured the more bizarre aspects of pop culture and the counterculture. His tone was often satirical, aimed at exposing the hypocrisy of New York social climbers, the literary establishment, and art dealers, for example. In one particularly biting essay titled "Radical Chic" (1970), Wolfe mocks the high-society guests of a party held for the militant Black Panthers, portraying them as shallow and hypocritical. But while Wolfe could be vicious when writing on his subjects, he also seemed fascinated and sometimes entranced by the people he wrote about.

Reflecting the spirit of the times, Wolfe wrote in what has been described as "breathless, syncopated prose," sometimes veering into a stream-of-consciousness style. He conveyed atmosphere and character by stringing together minute details and hyperbolic adjectives in commaless sentences. For example, he described Jimmy Carter as "an unknown down-home piney woods foot washing testifying share-it-brother soft-shelled holy roller."

An ardent advocate of New Journalism, Wolfe incorporated fictional techniques in non-fiction writing, rejecting the stance of detached objectivity traditionally associated with journalism. Instead, Wolfe attempted to reveal the "inner experience" of the people he profiled, sometimes writing what were supposedly their inner thoughts. Though the style was gaining in popularity and practitioners, Wolfe was attacked by critics for including uncheckable facts in his stories and embellishing them with inaccuracies.

Wolfe began dishing up more social analysis with his satirical observations, perhaps in an effort to be taken more seriously. For example, in "Radical Chic" Wolfe interrupts his satirical description of the party to put it into a historical context, giving examples of high society mixing with the lower classes in other eras. Some critics felt the analysis weakened his writing, and others claimed he was often just plain wrong in his historical comparisons.

In 1973, Wolfe began researching the space program, eventually focusing on the seven astronauts who were the first to fly to the moon. Six years later, *The Right Stuff* was published. In it, Wolfe describes how the seven men struggled to earn the right to fly the mission and how they were turned into heroes by the media and the public. The book became a bestseller and was eventually made into a Hollywood movie.

health foods, tai chi, Esalen, hypnotism, modern dance, meditation, Silva Mind Control, Arica, acupuncture, sex therapy, Reichian therapy, and More House — a smorgasbord course in New Consciousness.

Rubin also said he learned that "it's OK to enjoy the rewards of life that money brings," and that lesson later led him to join a Wall Street firm.

The New Religious Wave

For many, the search for meaning led to a renewed religious faith, or to a brand-new religious faith. In the seventies, spiritual seekers embraced a mind-boggling array of new religions, exotic faiths, cults, and versions of traditional religions. In the early seventies, a fundamentalist Christian movement known as the Jesus People spread across the country. Often reformed drug users, Jesus People were at first glance indistinguishable from hippies, with their long hair and communal lifestyle. The movement found its way into pop culture in the form of the Broadway musicals *Godspell* and *Jesus Christ Superstar.*

great concern to parents and gave rise to debates on religious freedom. By one estimate, more than ten million Americans became involved in cults in the seventies. Groups such as Hare Krishna and the Rev. Sun Myung Moon's Unification Church went to college campuses and large cities seeking to recruit new members. Converts often completely renounced their old lives, including school, jobs,

The more exotic religions that gained popularity in the seventies include the Church of Scientology, founded by science-fiction writer L. Ron Hubbard, and the Divine Light Mission of Guru Mararaj-ji, a fifteen-year-old who reportedly had sixty thousand followers in the United States. Mixed in with the new and exotic religions were a number of fringe religious cults, which caused

and family, and gave their money and themselves completely to their new religion. Many parents of cult members hired agents to kidnap their children and deprogram them to release them from the religion's hold.

By the late seventies, cult membership had fallen considerably, due in some cases to scandals involving cult leaders. Hubbard was accused of defrauding his followers by selling

Members of the Hare Krishna movement chant and dance in Minneapolis, Minnesota. Many young Americans tried out new beliefs in the search for self-awareness and to give meaning to their lives. Often they cut themselves off from their families and jobs and gave all they owned to their new religion.

Patty Hearst.

The enigmatic case of Patty Hearst was one of the most closely watched and heavily covered news stories of the seventies. Granddaughter of the publishing mogul William Randolph Hearst, Patty was born into a life of wealth and luxury. But on February 4, 1974, she was ripped from that life when she was kidnapped from her Berkeley, California, apartment. Two days later, the Symbionese Liberation Army claimed responsibility for abducting the nineteen-year-old. The SLA, a radical group determined to topple what they called the "fascist capitalist class," demanded that the Hearsts distribute $400 million in food to the poor as ransom for their daughter. Her father agreed to set up a $2 million giveaway program, but several weeks later, Patty sent a message saying that she had voluntarily joined the SLA and changed her name to "Tania," after a fellow revolutionary who had been killed.

The news came as a shock, but then an even more shocking event occurred. On April 15, Hearst participated with the SLA in an armed robbery of a San Francisco bank. Shortly afterwards, she sent a taped message in which she called her parents "pigs and clowns" and denied that she had been coerced into the robbery. The next month, five SLA members were burned to death when their hideout caught fire during a police raid. Patty, who had left the hideout before the raid, soon vanished after she and two SLA members went underground. After over a year of searching for her, the FBI arrested Hearst in September of 1975. But the raggedy-looking twenty-two-year old who appeared in court looked totally changed. She raised her fist in the air as a salute to her comrades and gave her occupation as "urban guerilla."

As she awaited trial in jail, however, Patty gradually changed back to the dutiful daughter of wealth. The Hearsts chose two high-priced lawyers to defend their daughter, who was now willing to testify against her former comrades. The central issue of the trial became whether or not Patty had been brainwashed or otherwise coerced into her illegal activities with the SLA. Psychiatrists argued for both sides, but in the end the jury was not convinced that she hadn't acted voluntarily, partly due to the fact that she invoked the Fifth Amendment (which allows defendants not to testify as witnesses against themselves) forty-seven times during her testimony.

Patty Hearst was convicted of bank robbery and sentenced to seven years in prison. After serving twenty-two months, however, President Carter commuted her sentence and she was freed on February 1, 1979. Public reaction was divided. Some people felt sympathy for Hearst, but others believed she was given "special justice" because of her family's wealth.

> *"The wilting flower child [has] blossomed into the Jesus Freak."*
>
> *Life* magazine

Patty Hearst (center) arrives for a court hearing in 1976.

Cult Loyalty Leads to Mass Death

them "e-meters" to measure their spiritual progress, the Mararaj-ji was implicated in a sex scandal, and the Rev. Moon was accused by a U.S. House of Representatives subcommittee of being a Korean spy.

In the late seventies, just as the wave of cults appeared to be ebbing, tragedy struck. In November of 1978, around 900 cult members died in a mass suicide in Jonestown, Guyana. As *Newsweek* magazine reported, "It was as if all the zany strains of do-it-your-self religion and personality-cult salvation that have built up in America had suddenly erupted with ghastly force."

The cultists were followers of Jim Jones, the mysterious founder of the People's Temple. In the beginning, the organization was known as a liberal, integrationist church that appealed to the poor, the disadvantaged, and African-Americans. With large followings in San Francisco and Los Angeles, Jones's organization won acclaim for operating drug rehabilitation and other social improvement programs. Jones gained political power as well, with his proven ability to deliver large blocks of votes, and by 1976, his support was being sought by Democratic vice-presidential candidate Walter Mondale and future first lady Rosalyn Carter.

But as Jones was gaining power, he was losing his mind. He became increasingly paranoid and egoman-

iacal, claiming to be Jesus Christ and demanding fanatical loyalty from his followers. With a vision of a Christian, Socialist utopia in mind, Jones and his followers founded Jonestown in the jungles of Guyana, South America. By 1978, however, accusations of torture and other abuses were being leveled against the People's Temple. U.S. Congressman Leo Ryan traveled to Jonestown to investigate, accompanied by a group of journalists. Jones and his followers did their best to present a picture of peaceful harmony to the visitors, but several cult members secretly asked Ryan to help them escape. When Ryan and his party attempted to leave with the defectors, they were attacked by armed cultists who killed Ryan and several others. Realizing that his utopian dream was unraveling, Jones gathered his followers together and made them drink from a deadly vat of Kool-Aid mixed with cyanide and

Mass suicide in Jonestown, Guyana. The People's Temple cult aimed to create a Christian, Socialist paradise in the jungles of South America. Around 900 of its members, both adults and children, died, forced to drink poison by their leader Jim Jones.

Pope John Paul II visited the U.S. in October 1979 and received a warm welcome from enthusiastic crowds who lined the streets across the country to see him. No previous pope had travelled as widely and courted publicity as effectively as John Paul II.

tranquilizers. Grisly scenes from the mass suicide were soon splashed on televisions and newspapers around the world.

What caused the rise of cults and fringe religions in the seventies? According to some social scientists, society was changing so quickly that connections to family, community, and church were breaking down, and people were searching for something to fill the void. But not everyone looking for meaning in their lives turned to cults or est. Towards the end of the seventies, an increasing number of people were returning to traditional religions. Jimmy Carter's open profession of his Baptist faith was refreshing to many Americans. Whereas "announcing for Jesus" and claiming a renewed religious faith was considered fatally "unhip" a decade ago, more and more celebrities and public figures were doing just that in the late seventies. In 1979, millions of Americans enthusiastically welcomed

Pope John Paul II as he made his first visit to the United States. The pope extolled traditional moral beliefs and urged the nation's young to resist "temptations, fads and every form of mass manipulation." To many Americans, and not only Catholics, the pope was a symbol of hope and stability in the midst of such turbulent times.

The Bicentennial and the Revival of Patriotism

Another symbol of hope in the seventies was the bicentennial celebration of 1976. By the mid-1970s, Americans were deeply in need of a reason to celebrate. The Vietnam War, the Watergate scandal, the oil embargo, and "stagflation" (see chapter 9) had battered and bruised the image of the United States, and patriotism was growing harder and harder to come by. But, as the two hundredth anniversary of the Declaration of Independence approached, Americans saw an opportunity for healing, and for pulling together to celebrate the enduring promise of their country.

Unfortunately, marketing experts also saw an opportunity in the bicentennial — an opportunity for exploiting the swelling patriotic sentiment for big bucks. By the time the Fourth of July rolled around, proud citizens could express their love of country by purchasing anything from a "Spirit of '76" lamp to a bicentennial bikini. The head of the American Revolution Bicentennial Administration, John Warner, was so successful at arranging corporate tie-ins to the celebration that he was labeled "Mr. Buy-Centennial." The commercialization of the bicentennial offended many Americans, but it was not enough to spoil the party.

When July 4, 1976, finally arrived, people all over the country commemorated the bicentennial with celebrations both light-hearted and serious. Residents of the town of George, Washington, baked a sixty-square-foot cherry pie, and in Sheboygan, Wisconsin, 1,776 frisbees were sent sailing. In Chicago, Detroit, and Miami, over ten thousand people were naturalized as U.S. citizens in mass ceremonies, while elsewhere patriots waited in line for hours to view the two-hundred-year-old Declaration of Independence. One of the most spectacular celebrations took place in New York City, where hundreds of tall sailing ships, including sixteen of the world's largest, glided up the Hudson River. Despite the debates over commercialization and the uncertain future of their fragmenting country, Americans made the bicentennial a memorable and meaningful celebration. As President Ford observed, "Something wonderful happened. A spirit of unity and togetherness deep within the American soul sprang to the surface in a way that we had almost forgotten."

A patriot decides to paint a giant American flag on the wall of his house as part of the 1976 bicentennial celebrations.

CHAPTER 7
Pop Culture: Anything Goes

From the Bland to the Bizarre

Bob Marley was the leading performer of Jamaican reggae music. Reggae originated in the mid-1960s as a mixture of African-American pop, and African-Jamaican styles. The lyrics are often about social discontent and Rastafarianism, a religious movement whose followers believe that Ethiopian emperor Haile Selassie was divine and a savior.

Mention other decades and certain images and sounds come to mind. For the twenties, it's flappers and swinging jazz. The fifties conjure up sock-hops and poodle skirts, and the sixties were a time of flower children and psychedelic rock. By contrast, the seventies seem to have no solid cultural identity. On the one

hand, it seemed to be a time of bland conformity, with "easy listening" music from the Carpenters and the wide-lapeled, polyester leisure suits of disco. On the other hand, it was a period of bizarre experimentation, of towering platform shoes, and of rock star David Bowie dressed as an alien named Ziggy Stardust. The conflicting images convey the uncertain, confused mood of the nation in the seventies as people tried to feel their way in a rapidly changing, seemingly chaotic world.

Judging from the rise of nostalgia, especially for the fifties, many Americans were sick and tired of tumultuous times. The successes of the movie *American Graffiti*, the television show "Happy Days," and the Broadway musical *Grease* all revealed a longing to return to what many remember as a simpler time, a time of innocence and hope, before Vietnam and Watergate changed everything. But despite this penchant for rehashing a romanticized past, the seventies did breed some very exciting new developments in both pop culture and the arts.

The Break-up of Rock 'n' Roll

As *Rolling Stone* writer Steve Pond sees it, rock music faced two major problems in the seventies. For one thing, "rock 'n' roll simply wasn't dangerous anymore." In the fifties and sixties, rock had been the music of rebellion, and at least half of its allure for the younger generation was seeing how much it upset their parents. But by the seventies, rock had been around long enough that it was established; it was a business, and as a result, it seemed to lose its momentum as a cultural force.

"The other problem," says Pond, "was that rock had no center." Previously, one or two rock 'n' roll icons had provided a driving force behind the music scene, influencing others and unifying legions of fans. But the seventies were marked by the break-up of The Beatles and the death of Elvis Presley. Instead of moving in one general direction, rock music splintered into a wide variety of distinct genres, each with its own superstars. While groups such as the Allman Brothers Band developed a blues- and country-influenced style called southern rock, David Bowie and others invented "glam-rock," characterized by elaborate makeup, glittery costumes, and concerts filled with special effects. Jamaican reggae music gained a huge following in the U.S., thanks in large part to the music of Bob Marley, and soul flourished through the great talents of Stevie Wonder and Marvin Gaye.

In the late seventies, two styles of music that couldn't be more opposed to each other took hold in the United States, though one was much more commercially successful than the other. Born in the urban nightclub scene, "disco fever" spread across the country, helped in large part by the movie *Saturday Night Fever*, featuring John Travolta tearing up the dance floor in a white three-piece suit. Much to the disgust of hard-core rock fans, disco's danceable beat and slick sound attracted a huge following

of people who eagerly learned to "do the hustle." On the other end of the spectrum was punk rock, a loud and angry form of music imported from the disaffected youths of Britain. The best known punk band was the Sex Pistols, who exemplified the messy musicianship and the self-destructive tone that were trademarks of the music. With their safety-pin pierced noses and spiked hair, punk rockers brought back the spirit of rebellion to rock music with a vengeance.

In response to the wide variety of very different styles of music, radio stations were divided into specialized formats, each appealing to a specific group of listeners. Pop music fans knew which stations would give them the latest Elton John songs, and hard rockers knew where on the dial to find Led Zeppelin. The exclusive radio formats made perfect marketing sense, but they also reflected a society that was growing increasingly fragmented.

The Power of Television

By 1970, television already overshadowed all other forms of media, but during the decade, it became even more pervasive, reaching more people than ever before. Advances in satellite communications allowed images to be beamed to and from locations around the globe. In 1972, a record one billion people from all over the planet were able to join in the same experience when they all tuned in to watch the Munich Olympics. Other advances in technology include the minicam, which made immediate, on-the-spot news coverage more available, and slow-motion instant replay, which gave a

"Today, accountants look like Shakespearean actors, hair stylists wear short hair, clothes designers dress conservatively ... an orthodontist comes on looking like a cowboy .... Everybody's into reverse role playing."

John Weitz, fashion designer

new dimension to sports on television.

Television news also changed dramatically for the worse in the seventies, most critics would say. Media observer Ron Powers, for example, says that in the seventies, television

"All in the Family" was a comedy that dealt with the serious issues of the day, from the differing viewpoints of members of the argumentative Bunker family. It first appeared on TV screens in 1971 and became a big hit with the public.

news, especially local news, veered from journalism into show business. According to Powers, the disturbing trend began in the late sixties, when more people than ever before began tuning in to television news to witness such dramatic, visual events as the Vietnam War, student protests, and street riots. The huge growth in audience thrust TV news into, as

Powers puts it, "the heady realm of profitable programming."

In a quest for even higher ratings and still more profits, station managers turned to news consultants, whose job it was to find out how to maximize the audience appeal of the news. In other words, the purpose of TV news shifted from telling people what they needed to know to giving them what they wanted. Apparently, people no longer wanted in-depth coverage of important, complex social issues. What they wanted instead were stories about flying saucers, runaway wives, and sexual fantasies, all reported by good-looking newscasters with "personality." The trend was especially troubling in light of a 1974 poll that indicated that, for the first time, a majority of Americans were relying on television for their news rather than newspapers.

Just as the marketing experts changed TV news, they also influenced prime-time programming. In an attempt to appeal to the eighteen-to-forty-nine age group, who supposedly had the greatest purchasing power, the networks began producing programs with "relevance," which was one of the buzzwords of the youth movement. Marketing analysts told the networks that what young people wanted was programming that dealt with the real issues they faced in a changing world. The networks once again responded. In 1971, CBS premiered a new show with the following introduction:

The program you are about to see is "All in the Family." It seeks to throw a humorous spotlight on our frailties, prejudices and concerns. By making them a source of laughter, we hope to show in a mature fashion, just how absurd they are.

The show, which became one of the most popular of the decade, revolved around the middle-aged, blue-collar worker, Archie Bunker, who was a confirmed bigot, male chauvinist pig, and old-fashioned patriot. Spouting off absurd right-wing theories and hilarious malapropisms, Archie went toe-to-toe with his feminist daughter and his liberal, long-haired son-in-law. Though the show was unmistakably a comedy, it dealt with such serious issues as racism, Vietnam, and the women's movement, thereby forging new territory for television.

Another television breakthrough of the seventies was "Saturday Night Live," a late-night comedy show featuring the irreverent humor of the "Not Ready for Prime Time Players." Every Saturday night, millions tuned in to watch Chevy Chase mimic President Ford's clumsiness or to see John Belushi perform his version of *Saturday Night Fever* dressed as a samurai warrior. No topic was safe from satire, and in the skeptical era of Watergate, Americans loved it.

As part of the new, relevant programming, television began reflecting the growth of ethnic pride in the seventies. After decades of shows featuring all-white, usually middle-class casts, ethnic variety began making its way onto the TV screen. Some of the more successful ethnic comedies were "Sanford and Son," about an African-American father-son team who owned a junk yard in Watts; "Good Times," which focused on a black family living in a Chicago housing project; and "Chico and The Man," which revolved around the relationship between a young Latino mechanic and the crabby old proprietor of the garage, who was white. Though the programs attracted large

audiences, they also drew a good deal of criticism from people who objected to the stereotypical aspects of some of the characters.

One of the most phenomenally popular television programs of the seventies was the miniseries "Roots," based on the bestselling book by Alex Haley, which traced his search into his family's genealogy. For eight consecutive nights in 1977, millions of Americans gathered around their TV sets to watch the gripping drama, which began with the kidnapping of a young African named Kunta Kinte

"Roots" was a 1977 TV miniseries, running for eight consecutive evenings, based on the prize-winning bestseller by Alex Haley. It is the story of an African slave, played by LeVar Burton, and his descendants. The program made many white people more sympathetic to African-Americans and sparked a widespread interest in genealogy. A sequel to "Roots" was televised in 1979.

Alex Haley. (1921-1992)

In the introduction to his Pulitzer Prize-winning book, *Roots: The Saga of an American Family*, Alex Haley explained that he was motivated to tell his story in part because "preponderantly the histories have been written by the winners." Through twelve years of genealogical research, Haley sought to tell the story from the other side.

After six years of lecturing all over the country about his search into his family's history, Haley finally saw his book published in October of 1976. It instantly became the top bestseller in the nation, and Haley became a public hero. When the book was produced as a television miniseries, Haley's star rose even higher. In 1979, the sequel to "Roots" was broadcast, titled "Roots: The Next Generation."

Though *Roots* was tremendously popular with the public, reviewers criticized Haley's use of "faction," a mixture of fact and fiction, to tell his story. A British journalist and several genealogists checked into Haley's research and reported many factual errors and inaccuracies. Still, Haley stood by the symbolic truth of his work, and several critics came to his defense, claiming that the factual details were not as important as the vivid, truthful portrayal of life in slavery. Haley was credited with correcting earlier myths about slavery by affirming the importance of family and African culture in the lives of slaves. In addition, Roots sparked a widespread interest in genealogy, which was encouraged by Haley, who even donated $100,000 of his earnings from the book to the Kinte Foundation to provide guidance for people researching their own roots.

Perhaps more threatening to Haley's reputation was a charge of plagiarism leveled by Harold Courlander, author of *The African*, who claimed that Haley lifted a passage from his book. Haley settled out of court for half a million dollars. Despite the challenges to Haley's research and sources, his work still stands as a powerful portrayal of the triumph of human will, the importance of family heritage, and the African-American experience.

into slavery and ended with his descendants gaining freedom after the Civil War. The program had such a powerful impact that it revived an interest in African-American history and motivated thousands of Americans to trace their own roots. A number of polls conducted after the miniseries indicated that many white viewers felt more sympathetic to the plight of blacks in the United States after watching "Roots." Though whether or not those feelings were translated into behavior is debatable, "Roots" is still a testament to the power of television.

"Sesame Street" and the Rise of Public Television

In the mid–1960s, critics of commercial television began a crusade for an alternative broadcasting outlet. In response, the Corporation for Public Broadcasting was formed in 1967. Funded in part by the federal government, the Public Broadcasting Service (PBS) really began taking off in the seventies.

One of the most popular PBS programs offered a fresh approach to educational television for preschoolers — "Sesame Street." Reflecting the egalitarian spirit of the times, "Sesame Street" featured a multiethnic, multiracial cast and was set in a friendly urban neighborhood. It also featured creator Jim Henson's Muppets, colorful, comical puppets that appealed to adults as well as children. Using a fast-paced mix of skits, games, and songs, "Sesame Street" sought to make learning fun. Parents were amazed to find their children glued to the TV set when "Sesame Street" came on, and one study showed that children who watched the program for six weeks were better able to identify letters, associate letters with sounds, and recognize and sort shapes than were children who hadn't watched the show. But critics were worried that "Sesame Street" was cultivating a new generation of TV addicts. Nevertheless, "Sesame Street" became so successful that it was translated and broadcast in countries all over the world.

Despite the success of "Sesame Street" and other programs, including the British series "Upstairs, Downstairs," PBS was still struggling in the early seventies. The Nixon administration, stung by investigative PBS reports on the Vietnam War and the FBI, cut back funding for public broadcasting. But then, in an ironic twist, it was the actions of Nixon's administration that inadvertently saved PBS. As writer Erik Barnouw explains, "The Watergate hearings gave public television a new lease on life. Some of its stations gained the highest ratings in their history" when they began broadcasting the Senate hearings live.

At the Movies

Throughout the fifties and sixties, television steadily lured away movie audiences, raising fears that film was a dying media. But in the seventies, a wave of blockbusters, including some of the highest grossing films of all time, excited new interest in the movies. Technical innovations such as Panavision and Dolby sound also helped by making moviegoing a richer experience than ever before. Despite rapidly rising ticket prices, millions of people rushed to theaters to view the latest "must-see" movies, films such as *Jaws*, directed by Stephen Spielberg, and *The Godfather*, directed by Francis Ford Coppola, now considered classics.

Like television, many movies reflected the social turmoil that the nation underwent in the late sixties and seventies. The hellish experience of the Vietnam War and its shattering aftermath were the themes of several seventies movies, including *Coming Home*, *The Deer Hunter*, and *Apocalypse Now*. The turmoil of divorce, another problem in the forefront, was the subject of *An Unmarried Woman* and *Kramer v. Kramer*. *Network* dealt with the dangerous power of the media, and *The China Syndrome* played to growing fears about nuclear power. Reflecting the more liberal social mood of the times, censorship became less and less a factor

Martin Scorsese.

Among the talented young directors who emerged in the seventies, Martin Scorsese stands out for creating films that are original, powerful, and controversial. His style has been described as subjective realism, for he combines a documentary-like depiction of life in the real world with distorted, dreamy interludes that reveal the inner feelings of his characters. A recurrent theme in Scorsese's films is that of the outsider, and an atmosphere of violence often surrounds his characters.

Scorsese's first movie to gain widespread attention was *Mean Streets,* produced in 1973. Scorsese cowrote the script, which drew heavily on his experiences growing up in the Little Italy section of New York City. *Mean Streets* tells the story of a small-time criminal named Charlie, whose drive to move up in the Mafia is hampered by his relationship with his old friend Johnny Boy, a wild young hood played by the then-unknown Robert De Niro. The Mafia bosses not only want Charlie to stay away from Johnny Boy but also want him to give up his epileptic girlfriend. The vivid portrayal of life on the streets and of Charlie's inner struggle made the film a hit with most reviewers, including Pauline Kael, who called it "a true original of our period, a triumph of personal film-making."

Perhaps the movie that Scorsese is best known for, *Taxi Driver,* created a great deal of controversy when it was released in 1976. The film explores the alienation of urban life through the story of Travis Bickle, an ex-marine cab driver played by Robert De Niro. Bickle is deeply disgusted by the decadence of New York City, and his rejection by a beautiful woman hastens his descent into madness. He is a deadly time bomb waiting to go off, and in the climax of the film, he does just that. The horrifying violence at the end of the movie was too much for some reviewers, but others agreed with critic David Sterritt, who called *Taxi Driver* "the nastiest masterpiece in years."

Always willing to take risks, Scorsese experimented with a variety of different genres. The 1977 film *New York, New York* is based on the Hollywood-style musicals of the 1940s, and the 1978 film *The Last Waltz* is the first thirty-five millimeter rock movie, documenting The Band's last concert.

in movies. As a result, nudity, profanity, and graphic violence became commonplace.

One genre of filmmaking that was a unique product of the seventies was the disaster movie. Perhaps reflecting the jittery atmosphere created by such real-world catastrophes as Vietnam, Watergate, and the economy, disaster movies usually featured a few regular people who become heroes by keeping their head while the world around them goes haywire. Some of the movies also seemed to reveal a grow-ing suspicion of modern technology, such as *The Towering Inferno,* in which a high-rise catches fire due to faulty design, trapping hundreds of helpless people. Others centered around natural disasters. Following environmentalists' warnings about the dangers of taking the natural world for granted, perhaps the popularity of *Earthquake* and *The Poseidon Adventure* represented Americans' revived respect for the environment. Whatever the reason, moviegoers in the seventies couldn't seem to get enough of the disaster movies. One of the most successful was *Airport*, which spawned three sequels.

Perhaps it was simply the escapism of disaster movies that made them so popular. Many Americans went to the theater merely to flee the real world for two hours, and the movies did not let them down. Hollywood discovered the formula for blockbuster success by combining spectacular special effects with simple, good-versus-evil story lines. The most successful movie of the decade was *Star Wars,* directed by George Lucas,

a futuristic fairy tale that relied on the tried-and-true techniques of cliff-hanger dramas and plot elements from classic myths. The catch phrase of the film, "The force be with you," also struck a note with followers of the new consciousness movement.

Star Wars was one example of a growing trend: As the decade progressed, blockbusters increasingly dominated the movie industry. By the seventies, many of the major studios had been purchased by huge conglomerates, and as a result, movies became even more of a big business

Star Wars, *directed by George Lucas, was the most successful movie of the decade. It was a futuristic adventure with spectacular special effects, features emphasized in this advertisement for the movie.*

Luis Valdez.

The son of migrant farm workers, Luis Valdez developed an early passion for the theater. Beginning in the sixties, he channeled that passion into La Causa, César Chávez's struggle to empower migrant workers through his United Farm Workers union. Using nonactors and with virtually no resources, Valdez organized a theater troupe called El Teatro Campesino, which traveled to protest rallies, farm fields, college campuses, and even to Washington, D.C., to teach audiences about La Causa through entertainment.

After the theater troupe established a permanent home in San Juan Bautista, California, Valdez was commissioned to write a play concerned with the history of Los Angeles. He chose to focus on the zoot suit riots of the early forties between Chicano gang members and soldiers and sailors, and the Sleepy Lagoon murder trial of 1942, which resulted in the unjust indictment of twenty-two young Chicanos. The combination of history told from the Chicano point of view and the colorful atmosphere of the big band era made the musical a smash hit in Los Angeles. The play was not as well received in the East Coast, however, where New York critics were less familiar with the history of zoot suiters. (Zoot suits featured wide pant legs and tight cuffs under long coats and wide-brimmed hats, which were worn by young Mexican-Americans.) Zoot Suits was later made into a movie, however, which received favorable reviews and launched Valdez's career as a film director and screenwriter.

As a leading Latino cultural figure in the U.S., Valdez took his responsibility seriously. He was concerned with the danger that Chicano culture would be lost in the melting pot of the United States. In an effort to keep that heritage alive, Valdez produced a series called "Corridos" for public television in the seventies. "Corridos" was based on the Mexican folk ballad tradition that carried news from town to town in the form of songs.

Valdez's work also revealed his belief that art and politics are inevitably intertwined. "We can't move politically," he said, "until we have artists who can express what the people are thinking and feeling."

than they were before. As profit making became the overriding goal, the movie industry began producing fewer movies and doing everything possible to ensure that the movies they did produce were financial successes. Movie studios launched huge, expensive advertising campaigns to create excitement over upcoming films. Then, to cash in on that excitement as much as possible, merchandising schemes were developed to offer fans their favorite movie characters on everything from coffee mugs to T-shirts to lunch boxes.

The surprise smash hit of the decade, however, was not a product of the blockbuster formula. Written and directed by an unknown actor named Sylvester Stallone, who also starred in the film, *Rocky* mixed both realism and escapism and came up with a winning combination. Set with gritty realism in a poor neighborhood of Philadelphia, *Rocky* told the story of an unknown boxer with a heart of gold whose life seems to be going nowhere. Everything changes when the heavyweight champ gives Rocky a chance at the title as part of a bicentennial publicity stunt. Though Rocky loses the fight, he achieves his personal goal of going the distance. Part of the reason for the tremendous success of *Rocky* is that it tapped into the bicentennial spirit that was rising in the country as Americans searched for reasons to be hopeful. *Rocky* reaffirmed the American dream with its "little-guy-makes-good" plot and gave Americans something they desperately needed in the seventies — a hero.

On a Literary Note

As *Rocky* exemplifies, the American dream is a prevalent theme in American culture. Many writers in the seventies explored the subject as well, and most found the dream to be a flawed myth. For example, the works of John Updike, one of the most popular authors of the decade, depict characters trying to find meaning in a society that is spiritually empty and in a state of moral decay. Kurt Vonnegut also explored the loneliness of contemporary society and the power-hungry materialism that pervades it. In novels such as *Breakfast of Champions, Slapstick,* and *Jailbird,* Vonnegut gets his messages across with an absurd brand of black humor, often incorporating elements of fantasy and other experimental techniques, such as inserting himself into the story.

John Updike.

John Updike first gained popularity in the sixties for his witty, artfully detailed novels and short stories. Many of his writings appeared in the *New Yorker* magazine, which gained him a large following. Critical opinion is divided over Updike. He has been accused of being too cute, and of writing superficial stories that merely show off his technique. Though some of Updike's stories are about seemingly unimportant events, they are often indicative of deeper themes. Updike's most serious works explore the struggle to balance physical desires with spiritual needs and vividly describe the confusion of life in contemporary society.

One of Updike's most successful novels of the seventies is *Rabbit Redux*, a sequel to his earlier novel, *Rabbit Run*. Rabbit is a conservative suburbanite, but his world is turned upside down when the turmoil affecting the nation in the late sixties, when the novel is set, infects his own life. After his wife has an affair and leaves him, Rabbit hooks up with an eighteen-year-old girl, who has run away from her rich family, and with her friend, a militant, black Vietnam vet. The two radicals continually challenge Rabbit's long-held belief in the American dream, and the liaison eventually ends in disaster. Throughout the novel, images from the 1969 moon landing, which provides a backdrop for the action, are interspersed. The bleak emptiness of outer space is implicitly equated with the loneliness of the main characters.

One aspect of Updike's writing that has made him popular with readers is his ability to combine serious themes with a witty, sometimes even playful, style. In *A Month of Sundays*, published in 1974, Updike tells the story of a minister who is having a crisis of faith. He has just been sent to a desert retreat after it was revealed that he had been having affairs with members of his church. The novel is in the form of his diary, which he believes is being read by the manager of the retreat, Ms. Prynne. As he writes in the journal, he addresses notes directly to "the reader," which, though meant to be Ms. Prynne, has the effect of pulling the actual reader directly into the story. It is this ability to involve readers in his explorations of life that has made John Updike such a popular and influential writer.

Joyce Carol Oates was one of an increasing number of talented women writers who made important contributions to American literature in the seventies. Also concerned with the search for spiritual life in modern society, Oates's short stories and novels were often infused with graphic violence and bizarre characters, making her a somewhat controversial writer. One of the strongest voices to emerge in the seventies was Toni Morrison, an African-American writer whose novels are filled with the rhythms, folklore, and enchantment of black culture. A common theme in Morrison's work is the oppressiveness of traditional roles and societal expectations. In *The Bluest Eye*, for example, she tells the story of a young black girl who goes mad because she cannot meet society's ideals of blond, blue-eyed beauty and an orderly family life. It is a powerful novel and just one example of the many perspectives on modern American life provided by the literature of the seventies.

Art and Architecture

The seventies was a confusing and exciting period in the world of art. In part, the confusion was in reaction to the avant-garde movement of the sixties, when pop art, minimalism, and conceptual art took ever-greater risks as they rejected traditions and overturned assumptions about art. Some avant-garde movements continued into the seventies, including so-called earth art, a form that combined environmental and minimalist ideas on a large scale. Michael Heizer is one seventies' artist who, through earth art, sought to break all of the rules regarding mass, time, size, and space that had governed sculpture for over three thousand years. For example, in a work entitled *Double Negative* (1969-70), Heizer removed twenty-four thousand tons of earth and rock from the Virgin River Mesa in Nevada to create sculpture within the earth.

But the avant-garde in the seventies was no longer the dominating force it had been. In fact, many art critics felt the avant-garde had run out of room. After all, now that Andy Warhol's painting of a giant soup can had been accepted as art, where were the new frontiers? What taboos were left to be smashed?

Though there was no single dominant force, art in the seventies took many different, exciting forms, such as a new interest in illusionism, art that sought to surprise viewers and move them to question their interpretation of reality. One stunning example is a 1978 sculpture by Wendy Taylor entitled *Brick Knot,* which appears to be a solid brick column that has somehow been tied into a knot. Super realism was another technique that engaged and fooled the senses. Artist Chuck Close, for example, painted close-up portraits that imitated the qualities of a photograph. One area of the face, the eyes and nose perhaps, appeared in sharp focus while the hair, chin, and shoulders were not.

The influence of the women's movement was evidenced by an increase in recognition of women artists as well as in subject matter. One of the best-known feminist artists of the decade was Judy Chicago. (Born Judy Cohen Gerowitz, she adopted a feminist practice of using her birthplace as her last name.) Chicago's most famous work was the

Frank Stella was one of the leaders of the minimal art movement, which emphasized simplicity, objectivity, color, shape, and structure. The picture here, Targowica III *(1973), is composed of cardboard, felt, and paint.*

Dinner Party Project, a five-year collective project that paid homage to major women figures in the history of Western culture. The project was described as a feminist *Last Supper,* with thirty-nine place settings. The *Dinner Party Project* was typical of seventies' art in that it emphasized a renewed respect for craft skills, in this case the traditional women's crafts of china painting and embroidery. The project's emphasis on a political theme (feminism) was also typical of seventies art. Ecology and antiwar sentiments were other themes expressed through art.

Just as the avant-garde movement slowed down in the seventies, the modern movement also lost ground in the world of architecture. The stripped-down steel and glass structures built in the fifties and sixties were now coming under attack for what critics called an "anonymous

Twyla Tharp.

"Dancing is like bank robbery," said Twyla Tharp. "It takes split second timing." The statement reveals both the precision and the wit that made Tharp one of the most innovative — and popular — choreographers in American dance.

Tharp formed her own dance troupe in 1965 and quickly won critical acclaim for her daring, avant-garde dances, which were performed without music on bare stages or in museums. In the seventies, however, Tharp began choreographing dances that showed more awareness of the audience, and as a result, she attracted more than the usual dance aficionados. The 1971 performance of *Eight Jelly Rolls*, set to the jazz music of Jelly Roll Morton, was the first example of Tharp's so-called pop ballets.

Tharp's imaginative style stems from her fascination with human movement in all its forms. Anything is fair game: classical ballet phrases, a baseball pitcher's windup, tap dance, and even Groucho Marx's famous bent-kneed walk. But perhaps what most delighted and astounded audiences was her ability to intelligently and elegantly blend such a wide variety of elements into what writer Amanda Smith called "witty pieces of flowing, liquid architecture."

One of Tharp's most popular and successful dances was *Deuce Coupe*, a ballet choreographed to the surfer-rock music of the Beach Boys. In it, a sole ballerina precisely performs the classic ballet steps surrounded by other dancers who are wildly doing the bugaloo, the jerk, and other popular dances of the sixties and early seventies. In the background, graffiti artists create their own art on a rolling backdrop.

Though Tharp's dynamic works excited new interest in dance, she was accused by some critics of trying too hard to please the audience, of being too "modish." In response to such criticism, Tharp said, "I think that's just people not understanding that art is a human function, and thinking that art is something only God does, or the gods do. . . . Somehow it's got to be held special, sacred in a corner, and . . . if you're not equally reverential, serious, and pompous about it, well, then you're not a great artist. Who needs that?"

functionalism." Increasingly architects were incorporating a warmer, more humanistic approach in their designs, concerned with the feelings of the people who would be using the buildings. For example, a Chicago library for the blind and disabled designed by Stanley Tigerman (1976-78) features built-in furniture so the blind will always know where it is. The interior is also designed entirely in soft or round shapes to prevent accidents and to help guide the users.

The loss of confidence in the modern movement was also expressed in a renewed respect for historical architecture. In cities and towns across the country, rising support for historical preservation saved many old buildings from being demolished or remodeled. In 1978, the Supreme Court ruled that New York City had the right to prevent remodeling of the impressive and historic Grand Central Station on the grounds that "these buildings and their workmanship . . . embody precious features of our heritage . . . [and] serve as examples of quality for today."

Fashion Plates

Many people consider fashion one of the most reliable indicators of society's changing attitudes. During the seventies, many of the styles that were considered the domain of the radical youth culture in the sixties were incorporated into the mainstream. In the sixties, most high school students still dressed rather conservatively, but in the early seventies, the hippie look caught on, with its emphasis on the casual and rejection of anything uptight or traditional. Long hair also became more acceptable, and as it did so, it lost some of its symbolism. Whereas hippies wore long hair as a "freak flag" in the sixties, even patriotic southern boys were letting their hair grow in the seventies. A hairstyle that held onto its symbolism a little longer was the big afro, worn by African-Americans as a sign of black pride. The style of war protesters was also considered "hip" as khaki clothes with pseudomilitary badges sewn onto them became fashionable. Denim was the fabric of choice in the seventies as blue jeans, from bell bottoms to straight legs, became widely popular. In general, fashion became a lot more casual and informal in the seventies.

Around the mid-1970s, however, fashion trends that would undoubtedly be rejected by true hippies began to take hold. Soon not even blue jeans were safe from status symbolism as designer jeans caught on. Just a tiny label or an embroidered name on the back pocket set the wearer apart as one who could afford to spend an extra ten or twenty dollars on a pair of jeans. Sixties radicals would

These two pictures display the contrasting fashions of the 1970s. Hot pants hit the headlines in 1971. Here, on the left, a model also wears knee-length boots and a coat decorated with nuclear disarmament emblems. In contrast, the model on the right wears a tweed midi-suit of 1970, by Paris designer Louis Feraud.

probably also balk at the spread of commercialism evident in the craze for T-shirts bearing advertising for everything from running shoes to beer.

Nicknamed "Dr. J," Julius Erving was the most brilliant basketball player of the decade. Here the Philadelphia star attempts to block a shot by a member of the Buffalo Braves team.

Other T-shirt messages included political commentaries and quotes from popular TV characters such as the Fonz from "Happy Days." Another fashion fad was spawned by the health craze beginning to spread across the nation. Once worn only by true athletes, jogging suits became popular, even among people whose

most vigorous exercise was walking to and from the car.

For the woman trying to keep up with the latest fashion trends, it must have been a confusing decade. In the early seventies, hot pants were in style, which seemed to be the next step after miniskirts. Worn with thigh-high boots or platform shoes, hot pants were supposed to make women's legs look longer. But in the second half of the decade, the "Annie Hall" look caught on, named after Woody Allen's 1977 movie. The style incorporated traditional men's fashions, such as derby hats, tweed jackets, and neckties, which were worn with baggy pants and skirts. The Annie Hall look was welcomed by feminists, who had grown tired of fashions they felt turned women into sex objects. The popularity of the style seemed to reflect the growing influence of the women's movement — or was it was just another passing trend?

The World of Sports

Among the stranger trends in sports in the seventies was the rise of rival leagues that dared to take on the long-established organizations. The World Football League was one short-lived example that featured such peculiar team names as the Chicago Fire and the Detroit Wheels. The World Hockey Association persuaded superstars Bobby Hull and Gordie Howe into joining the newly founded organization. The American Basketball Association was founded in 1967 but gained attention in the early seventies for its red, white, and blue ball and the dazzling play of "Dr. J," Julius Erving.

Muhammad Ali reappeared in the headlines in the seventies after charges of draft evasion were overruled in 1970. He returned to the ring to win back the heavyweight title from George Foreman in 1974 and, after losing it in 1978, regained it four months later to became the only man to ever win the world heavyweight title three times.

The 1972 Munich Olympics were a mixture of triumph and tragedy. American swimmer Mark Spitz became an instant hero by winning seven gold medals, but his feats were overshadowed when Palestinian terrorists kidnapped Israeli athletes in the Olympic village. The siege ended with a shootout and massacre at a West German airport that left eleven Israeli athletes, five terrorists, and one policeman dead.

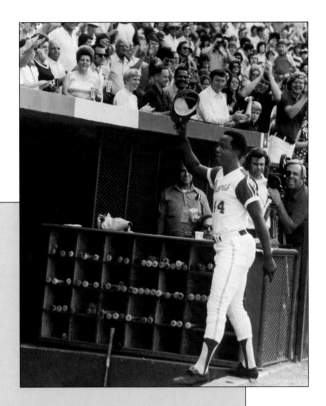

Henry "Hank" Aaron.

One of the first black ballplayers to play on white teams in the South, Hank Aaron was known as a quiet man with a powerful bat. Though he had consistently demonstrated his prowess at the plate, he did not attract much media attention and was considered by many to be the most underrated player in the major leagues.

By 1972, however, as Aaron approached 700 home runs, fans and sportswriters were waking up to the fact that he was likely to be the one to finally break Babe Ruth's long held record of 714 home runs. In the summer of 1973, the media turned its spotlight on "Hammerin' Hank" and kept it there as excitement began to build over "The Chase." But, along with the excitement, an ugly element of racism emerged. As Aaron closed in on Ruth's record, he began receiving hate mail and death threats from people who did not want to see an African-American man break Ruth's record. The FBI investigated the threats, and Aaron hired a bodyguard to protect him.

To Aaron, all of the attention and pressure to break the record was a burden. He insisted that to him, the more important achievement was when he reached three thousand runs-batted-in in 1970, a rare accomplishment that he felt demonstrated his consistency as a hitter. As for The Chase, Aaron said, "All I want is to be treated like a human being. I've said it until it's tiresome: I'm not trying to be another Babe Ruth. All I'm trying to do is play the game and earn a living and be a part of my team."

Finally, on April 8, 1974, Aaron hit his 715th home run in front of a multitude of cameras. The fans went wild. When two excited college students jumped on to the field and ran up to congratulate Aaron, he quickly pushed them away, unsure of their intentions.

Aaron was relieved to have the home run record behind him and be able to focus on the game again. At the end of the season, Atlanta traded Aaron to the Milwaukee Brewers, where he stayed for two seasons before retiring with 755 home runs and an incredible lifetime batting average of .305, ensuring him a place in the Baseball Hall of Fame.

Billie Jean King.

Undoubtedly one of the greatest women athletes of all time, Billie Jean King was not only a powerful tennis player but an important symbol of the women's movement in the seventies. Her fierce, aggressive style of play quickly moved her up through the ranks of tennis.

But as she gained prominence, she became increasingly outraged at the disparity between the prizes for men's and women's tournaments, and she began organizing other women players to demand a change. At the Italian Open in May of 1970, King discovered that first prize for the women's singles was $600, compared to $7,500 for men. "That's when I began thinking boycott," said King. ". . . There was no alternative. . . . Everywhere the ratio was insulting." King's efforts were remarkably successful, and in 1971, she became the first woman athlete to earn $100,000 in a single year.

In 1973, King accepted a challenge to play former national champion and avowed male chauvinist pig Bobby Riggs in what was hyped as "The Battle of the Sexes." A known hustler, Riggs sought to tap into the controversy surrounding the women's movement for big money. King only agreed to the match after fellow tennis champ Margaret Smith Court was badly beaten by Riggs, who boasted "No broad can beat me." In offices and homes all over the country, men and women placed bets on the match — sometimes for "who would do the dishes or carry out the garbage for the next month," remembers one writer. Despite the fact that Riggs was fifty-five and King was only twenty-nine and in excellent shape, Las Vegas odds were against her eight to five.

Though Riggs planned on psyching out King by creating a circus atmosphere around the match, King matched him gimmick for gimmick. After a group of buxom women pulled Riggs into the Houston Astrodome in a Chinese rickshaw, King was brought in on a Cleopatra-style litter carried by six brawny men. But then the two players got down to business as a record-breaking television audience tuned in to watch. King stunned the fans wearing "Pigs for Riggs" buttons by beating their hero in straight sets.

In the late seventies, after multiple knee surgeries and facing an aggressive young player named Chris Evert, King gave up major singles tournaments, opting instead to play with a league she established called World Team Tennis. But as the younger women players began moving up in tennis, they were well aware of their debt to the person who brought women's sports to the main stage.

Passing Fancies

Despite the many gloomy events of the seventies, or perhaps because of them, Americans managed to find plenty of ways to distract and amuse themselves. For the athletically inclined there was skateboarding, hang gliding, and jogging, a trend that reached all the way to the White House and President Jimmy Carter.

Among the more bizarre fads in the seventies was the craze for mood rings, which were filled with liquid crystals that changed colors according to the wearer's body temperature. The colors ranged from purple, which supposedly indicated happiness, to black, which was said to reveal tension. Apparently, within two years there were a lot of nervous people, for that's how long it took the crystals to wear out and turn black permanently. Pet rocks were another fad, the ultimate gag gift that even came with a care and training manual. But perhaps the wildest fad of the decade was streaking, which involved running at high speed in public places — without any clothes on. During the winter and spring of 1974, streakers showed up in the most unexpected places, including on the live Academy Awards broadcast. The fad was especially popular on college campuses, which seemed to indicate that the high-minded protests of the past decade were giving way to a party atmosphere.

President Carter jogs on the White House lawn. Jogging was a craze that began in the 1970s. As people became more self-aware, they took better care of their health. Jogging suits became a popular fashion and were worn by many people, even when they were not exercising.

CHAPTER 8
A Brave New World

Progress and Fear

The seventies was a period of amazing technological advances affecting almost every aspect of human life, including health, transportation, work, and leisure. Though many of the advances were greeted with eager excitement, they also gave rise to difficult questions, such as: What is an acceptable price for progress, both in terms of money and in risks to health and the environment? At what point does technology go too far in changing the human condition? As science and industry raced to make things stronger, bigger, faster, or more efficient and medical technology advanced, an increasing number of undesirable and unpredictable side-effects arose. The United States seemed to be in a love/hate relationship with progress as the irresistible urge to move forward combined with the fear of what lay ahead.

A New Age of Space Exploration

The splashdown of *Apollo 17* on December 19, 1972 marked the end of the Apollo moon exploration program. By the time the thrilling adventure that began with Neil Armstrong's "giant leap for mankind" in 1969 was over, six piloted flights had reached the moon. Astronauts had lugged back over eight hundred pounds of lunar rocks and left behind plaques, flags, a moon buggy, and their footprints. The Apollo program had been a source of great national pride, putting the Americans ahead of the Soviets in the space race. But twenty-five billion dollars later, the program was deemed too costly to continue, and piloted moon landings ceased. The decision was somewhat controversial. Astronaut Gene Cernan called the move "an abnormal restraint of man's intellect at this point in time."

But the end of Apollo did not mean the end of space exploration; it indicated a change in direction. As one scientist explained: "The age of excitement that ushered in man's televised exploration of the moon may well be over. But the earnest business of finding out more about the earth and solar system is just beginning. To accomplish the task, scientists are turning the finely honed tools of Project Apollo toward new tasks."

Those new tasks included the use of satellites to tell humankind more about its own planet, such as the condition of natural resources, the movement of ocean currents, and the behavior of weather patterns.

The largest project to follow Apollo, however, was *Skylab*, a $2.6 billion space station that was launched in May of 1973. The purpose of *Skylab* was to test the ability of humans to live and work in the weightlessness of outer space for prolonged periods. In each of the three phases of the *Skylab* mission, a three-man crew visited the space station as it orbited the earth. The last crew stayed in space for a

SPACE

For further information
see primary source entries
on pages

12: 1625-26, 1694-96

Apollo 17, *shown here on
lift-off in December 1972,
was NASA's last lunar
expedition. Scientists felt
that the expense of manned
flight was unnecessary, as
valuable information about
the solar system could be
obtained using unpiloted
spacecraft. During the
1970s, the* Mariner,
Pioneer, Viking, *and*
Voyager *craft sent back
data and exciting pictures of
Mercury, Venus, Mars, and
Jupiter.*

record-breaking eighty-four days,
returning in February of 1974.
Though *Skylab* provided the U.S. with
a vast amount of scientific information,
the abandoned space station came to a
degrading end when it reentered the
earth's atmosphere in 1979 and crashed
in an Australian desert.

Competition between the U.S.
and the USSR continued mainly in
the form of unpiloted missions to
explore earth's planetary neighbors. In
1975, the Soviet *Veneras 9* and *10*
spaceships soft-landed on Venus and
sent back astonishing pictures, the first
ever from the surface of that planet.

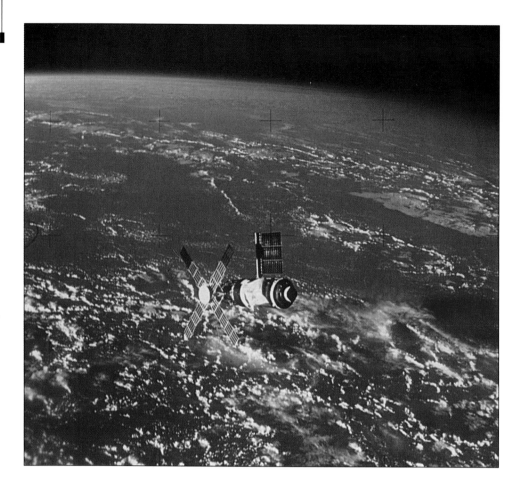

Skylab, *an earth-orbiting space station, was launched in May 1973 and was manned until February 1974. Here,* Skylab *can be seen against a background of the earth, with oceans and clouds clearly visible. In the 1970s, satellites were put into orbit to collect information about the earth itself, helping to discover how weather systems work and monitoring the planet's natural resources.*

In 1976, two U.S. spacecraft, *Viking 1* and *Viking 2,* soft-landed on Mars and tested for signs of life, to no avail. The competition between the two superpowers was temporarily set aside, however, and the spirit of détente reached into outer space in 1975, when the U.S. Apollo and the Soviet Soyuz spacecraft linked up while they were orbiting the earth.

Transportation: Setting Limits

Just as high costs put limits on the space program in the seventies, the oil crisis dramatically affected the transportation industry. As the price of gasoline continued to rise, the huge, powerful cars for which Detroit was famous fell out of favor with consumers. While American automakers were somewhat slow to respond to changing demands, Japanese manufacturers quickly jumped in to fill the void, providing cheap, fuel-efficient autos for the U.S. market. The influx of foreign cars was deeply threatening to the American auto industry.

Air travel was also affected by the oil crisis. After twenty years and hundreds of millions of dollars were spent in development, the world's first supersonic airliner, the Anglo-French Concorde, began service in 1976. Though the plane was considered a triumph of design and was able to whisk passengers from London to New York in just over three hours, it soon ran into some heavy turbulence. Not only was the Concorde inefficient to operate, it also made a loud noise as it broke the sound barrier, which led some countries to ban the aircraft from flying over them. In contrast, the Boeing 747 was very popular. Able to carry over three hundred passengers at a time, the jumbo jet made air travel more affordable. Even Cuba's Communist leader Fidel Castro admired this latest capitalist innovation. In August of 1970, a 747 jet carrying 379 passengers was hijacked to Havana. Castro boarded the plane and marveled at its capacity before allowing the pilot to take off for Miami.

Miniature Mania

At the same time as aircraft were growing larger, the electronics industry was headed in the opposite direction. Miniaturization seemed to be the wave of the future, for as electrical components were made smaller and smaller, electronic devices became more compact and affordable. Calculators are an excellent example. The first consumer calculators sold for about $150 in 1973, but by 1974, a smaller, more powerful calculator was selling for only $26.25. Miniature televisions arrived on the market in 1975, and in 1978, Sony announced its first miniature cassette player, the Walkman, which immediately became wildly popular.

The Computer Revolution

Miniaturization undoubtedly made the greatest impact in the computer industry. The first mainframe computers filled an entire room and were affordable only to the federal government and huge corporations. In the late sixties, the minicomputer was invented, which, though no longer room-sized, was still not exactly mini either. The size of a bookcase, minicomputers cost tens of thousands of dollars, but were at least affordable for medium-sized companies and

Toyota cars are unloaded at Castle Island, South Boston. Fuel-efficient Japanese cars capitalized on the oil price increases at a time when America was still making large, powerful, gas-guzzling autos.

Apple Computer president, John Sculley, is flanked by the cofounders of the company, Steve Jobs (left) and Steve Wozniak. The personal computer became a possibility with the introduction of the first microprocessor.

schools. Computer enthusiasts dreamed of a day when they would have their own personal computers instead of requiring permission for access to one machine shared by an entire school or laboratory. When the computer industry did not respond to their needs, they did it themselves. The personal computer industry was created entirely by hobbyists and computer "nuts" working outside the established corporations. Some of them became millionaires almost overnight.

The seeds for the personal computer revolution were planted in 1971, when the first microprocessor was patented. The equivalent of an entire computer processor on a small sliver of silicon, this device suddenly made the dream seem attainable. In 1975, the magazine *Popular Electronics* published an article describing the Altair, a microcomputer that could be built from a mail order kit. "It absolutely fired the imagination of everyone who was even remotely technically oriented, who wanted, sometime, to have a computer," said computer designer George Morrow. Soon after Altair's debut, a Harvard freshman named Bill Gates and his friend Paul Allen were contracted to write software for the computer. Within a few years, these cofounders of Microsoft would be millionaires. When a young computer wiz named Stephen Wozniak approached his employer, Hewlett-Packard, with the design for a personal computer, he found they weren't interested. So Wozniak teamed up with his friend Steve Jobs and began producing the computers in Jobs's garage. They named their fledgling company Apple Computer. The young entrepreneurs did not follow the usual procedure of business start-up. "We didn't do three years of research and come up with this concept," said Jobs. "What we did was follow our own instincts and construct a computer that was what we wanted." Their instincts proved to be right on the money.

Other Advances in Technology

Though most Americans in 1970 probably relegated robots to the realm of science fiction, by the end of the decade robotics was on its way to changing the face of industry in the United States. Unimation, one of the first robotics companies in the U.S., saw its sales jump from $2 million in 1967 to $14 million in 1972. Robotic arms, which could be programmed by computer and were small enough to work alongside humans, were introduced in auto assembly-lines and other industries to do material handling, welding, and light assembly

work. Though some workers feared losing their jobs to robots, business experts insisted robots were useful for performing boring, repetitive work and for doing dangerous jobs that

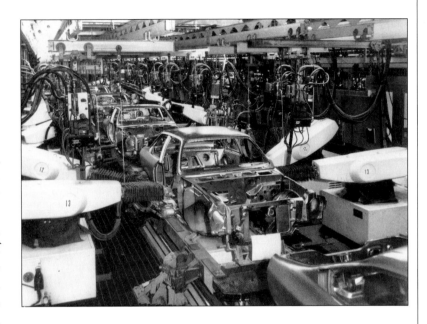

humans did not want to do. Besides, they argued, new jobs would be created as people were needed to program, manufacture, and maintain industrial robotics. If the U.S. did not keep up with the robotics movement, jobs would be lost to Japan and Germany, where the new technology was being enthusiastically embraced.

Lasers were another technological development that came into wide use in the seventies. Described as a beam of intensely pure light, the first laser was created in 1960. Able to make clean, fast cuts through everything from metal to rubber, lasers were put to use in the industrial world in the seventies. Doctors also found the accuracy of lasers to be helpful in eye surgery, and the first hologram, a three-dimensional image created by lasers, debuted in the seventies.

Robotic arms take over from humans on this General Motors assembly-line in 1970. By this time, automatic equipment had taken over most of the welding work in auto manufacturing.

New Life Through Transplants

"Have we the right to counteract, irreversibly, the evolutionary wisdom of millions of years, in order to satisfy the ambition and the curiosity of a few scientists? The future will curse us for it."

Dr. Erwin Chargaff, geneticist

In the medical field, the most exciting developments of the seventies were advances in heart and organ transplants. In 1967, Dr. Christiaan Barnard made history in Cape Town, South Africa, by transplanting the heart of a twenty-five-year-old woman killed in an accident into a fifty-five-year-old man. Though the patient died within three weeks, other doctors were enthusiastic about the possibilities, and a wave of heart transplants followed. The results were discouraging, however. By the end of 1970, 166 heart transplants had been attempted worldwide and only twenty-three recipients were still living — a mortality rate of 85 percent. The number of attempted transplants quickly dropped off.

But Dr. Norman Shumway did not give up. He realized that the problem with transplants was preventing the recipient's immune system from rejecting the new heart. "Everyone can do the surgery," he said. "The real problems start after the surgery." Shumway and his team devised a method for detecting the problems early. Caught soon enough, a newly developed drug therapy could be used to combat rejection. By the end of the decade, 70 percent of Shumway's patients were surviving for at least a year.

Techniques developed in the seventies also made organ transplants more successful. Kidney transplants especially became more common, but the availability of donor organs soon became a problem. Ethical dilemmas were also raised. For example, which patients should receive the few available organs, and is it wrong to take a patient off life-support systems so his or her organs can be donated?

"Playing God" and Test-tube Babies

Ethical dilemmas also seemed to go hand-in-hand with the incredible developments taking place in the area of genetic engineering. Though in the natural world species never interbreed, scientists found through recombinant DNA experiments that they were able to blend the genetic material of one species with the DNA of another to create an entirely new organism.

The experiments were highly controversial. While some scientists saw in genetic engineering the potential for new vaccines, more and better food, and answers to ecological problems, others feared that it amounted to "playing God." Some people feared the unpredictability of new organisms. What if a disease or virus were created and then spread out of control?

In response to such concerns, the scientific community called a moratorium on genetic experiments in 1973 while they explored the ethics involved. Some scientists, however, regarded the moratorium as an invasion of scientific freedom of research. In 1975, an international conference was held to debate the subject. The 150 biologists settled on a compromise: Research would continue but under stringent safeguards. In 1976, the National Institutes of Health issued a series of voluntary guidelines for future experimentation. But this action was not enough for some concerned scientists, including biologist

Liebe Cavalieri, who warned, "Only one accident is needed to endanger the future of mankind."

Nevertheless, genetic research continued. By the end of the decade, commercial researchers at General Electric had invented a living bacterial organism that could digest oil. The bacteria would presumably be helpful in cleaning up oil spills. In a very controversial 1980 ruling, the Supreme Court decided in favor of issuing a patent for such invented microorganisms.

Cloning experiments also raised fears and fired the imaginations of many science fiction writers. A clone (from the Greek word *klon*, meaning "twig") is a genetic copy of its parent, and is created through a single-parent method of reproduction. In the 1960s, a British biologist successfully cloned a frog, and experiments continued in the seventies, mainly on plants and other lower organisms. A 1978 book titled *In His Image* claimed that a baby boy had been cloned from a sixty-seven-year-old millionaire. Though the story was a hoax, some people wondered if humans were indeed next.

Confusion also surrounded the birth of the first test-tube baby on July 25, 1978. The birth of Louise Brown was made possible by a procedure called in-vitro fertilization, which involved removing an egg from the mother's ovary, fertilizing it with the father's sperm in a laboratory dish, and then implanting the embryo in the mother's uterus. Though the breakthrough gave hope to many infertile couples, it presented an ethical dilemma. Were humans interfering too much with nature? What if the highly delicate procedure resulted in a damaged baby? Who would be responsible? These and many other difficult questions associated with scientific advances placed focus on an increasingly important area of study — bioethics.

The Environmental Movement

For many people, the most frightening aspect of technological progress was what it was doing to the natural environment. Fears were raised in the sixties with the publication of Rachel Carson's influential book *Silent Spring*, which described the devastating effect that DDT and other chemicals were having on nature. A number of ecological disasters underscored those fears and focused the attention of an ever-growing number of Americans on the environment. The student protest movement quickly embraced the ecology crusade, but it wasn't only young people who were concerned. As Gaylord Nelson, a long-time environmentalist and senator from Wisconsin observed:

Everybody around the country saw something going to pot in their local areas, some lovely spot, some lovely stream, some lovely lake you couldn't swim in anymore.

After reading an article about the use of teach-ins to protest the Vietnam War, Nelson decided to organize a national teach-in on the environment, and the idea for Earth Day was born. On April 22, 1970, millions of people all over the country demonstrated their concerns and frustrations over threats to the environment. In San Francisco, a group poured oil into the reflecting pool in front of the Standard Oil offices to

"Society cannot continue to live on oil and gas. Those fossil fuels represent nature's savings accounts which took billions of years to form."

Buckminster Fuller

protest the oil slicks in offshore waters. In Tacoma, Washington, one hundred high school students called attention to auto pollution by riding horses down a highway.

According to the writer Philip Shabecoff, Earth Day marked "the dawn of the environmental era." The outpouring of public concern over

there was a huge outcry over the high costs of complying with the new regulations, but environmentalists countered that money would be saved as health risks and the need for clean-up operations were reduced.

Meanwhile, a stream of frightening ecological disasters proved the need for continued vigilance. In the Love Canal

Schoolchildren in St. Louis protest smog pollution from autos as part of the Earth Day campaign in 1970. In addition to countrywide demonstrations, lectures and debates on pollution and ecology were lively and frequent. During the 1970s, laws were passed to help protect the environment, and the Environmental Protection Agency was created.

the environment made politicians sit up and take notice, resulting in a flood of environmental legislation that was passed in the seventies. In 1970, President Nixon grouped together a number of federal public health organizations to create the Environmental Protection Agency. That same year, the Clean Air Act was passed, followed by the Federal Water Pollution Control Act in 1972, the Endangered Species Act in 1973, and the Federal Land Management Act in 1977. To carry out and enforce these laws, new agencies and boards were created, and law students began specializing in environmental law. A whole new industry was born, called pollution control. Among established industries

area of Niagara Falls, New York, a high rate of miscarriages, birth defects, and illness had residents concerned. When a 1978 article revealed that Hooker Chemicals had buried dangerous chemicals in the area, concern was soon translated into action. Lois Gibbs, a twenty-seven-year-old homemaker with two sick children, organized the Love Canal Homeowners Association. Though authorities repeatedly assured the residents that their community was safe, the grassroots movement's persistent efforts finally forced the government to act. At the cost of $17 million, the government eventually paid for the evacuation of all Love Canal families that chose to move.

One of the most serious threats

that galvanized a number of environmental groups was nuclear power. In the early seventies, a group calling itself Greenpeace was organized to halt the testing of nuclear devices in the Pacific Ocean. And, as the energy crisis made the idea of nuclear power generating plants more attractive, the antinuclear movement kicked into gear. Though proponents of nuclear power touted it as a clean, inexpensive source of energy, many people feared the potential for disaster should an accident occur. In addition, there was the problem of radioactive waste, which, once created by the reactor, continues to be radioactive almost indefinitely. The effects of radiation are not only dangerous to those directly in contact with it but to their offspring as well.

The proliferation of nuclear power plants was one target of a growing grassroots movement in the seventies. As the American public began to lose faith in the government's ability to respond to problems, more people began taking matters into their own hands. Gale Cincotta, head of an organization called National People's Action, said:

I keep hearing that everything's dead and there's no big cause since civil rights and the Vietnam War, but that's a myth. There's a neighborhood movement that started in the sixties. It's not as dramatic with everybody out in the streets, but it's steadily gaining strength in every city and state. The base was there and people reached the point where they just had to do something.

This boarded-up home is in the chemically contaminated Love Canal area, Niagara Falls, New York. Between 1942 and 1953, Hooker Chemicals stored over twenty-one thousand tons of hazardous waste in metal drums. The canal was then filled in and the land given to the city of Niagara Falls by the company. In the late 1970s, the drums leaked and the waste rose to the surface.

Many residents of the town of Seabrook, New Hampshire, reached that point when, despite strong opposition to a proposed nuclear power plant in their community, plans for the reactor went ahead. Beginning in plant. Six months later, in March of 1979, the concerns of antinuclear activists proved well-founded when the worst nuclear accident in U.S. history took place at Three Mile Island, near Harrisburg, Pennsylvania.

Karen Silkwood. (1946-1974)

When Karen Silkwood took a job at the Kerr-McGee nuclear processing plant in Cimarron, Oklahoma in 1972, she had no desire to become a symbol of the antinuclear movement. The twenty-six-year-old had dreams of becoming a scientist and left her husband and three children in Texas to follow that dream. But she soon became active in the Oil, Chemical and Atomic Workers International Union, and participated in a ten-week strike for higher wages and improved safety conditions.

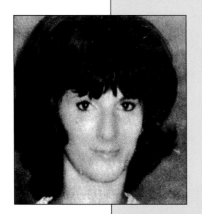

Silkwood's concerns over safety at Kerr-McGee, which processed fuel rods for nuclear reactors containing highly toxic plutonium, were intensified when she discovered in July of 1974 that she had been contaminated with radiation. In September of that year, she agreed to act as a spy for her union in an attempt to find evidence of unsafe and illegal practices at the plant. By the end of October, Silkwood told the union that she had enough evidence, and she planned to pass it on to a *New York Times* reporter.

One week before the scheduled meeting, however, Silkwood learned that she and her apartment had been mysteriously contaminated with plutonium. After a brief hospitalization, she was on her way to her rendezvous with the reporter when her car veered off the road and crashed into a culvert. Silkwood was killed. Union officials and antinuclear activists believed she was forced off the road, but the Justice Department determined there was not enough evidence for a case.

In 1976, Silkwood's family filed a multimillion dollar lawsuit against Kerr-McGee, charging that the plant was responsible for Silkwood's contamination. The case became the focal point of the antinuclear movement. Kerr-McGee attacked Silkwood's character, portraying her as an antinuclear fanatic who contaminated herself to dramatize the dangers of nuclear power. But testimony revealed that there were indeed unsafe conditions at the Cimarron plant, which had been closed down in December of 1975. Especially damaging was the acknowledgement that forty pounds of plutonium were missing. The jury awarded $10.5 million to Silkwood's estate — the harshest penalty ever assessed a U.S. corporation by a trial court. Suspicion continues to surround the cause of Silkwood's accident.

1976, residents adopted the peaceful protest methods of the civil rights movement, such as sit-ins, to block construction. Their campaign gained national attention. In 1977, over fourteen hundred protesters were arrested at Seabrook. Finally in 1978, the Nuclear Regulatory Commission decided to halt construction on the A failure in the plant's cooling system caused a leak of radioactive gases, and most of the surrounding area had to be evacuated. A later study revealed that the reactor was within one hour of a meltdown, which could have caused thousands of deaths. The near-disaster gave even more momentum to the antinuclear movement.

Small Is Beautiful versus the Global Corporation

Escalating threats to the environment led many people to question how the world had come to this point and what, if anything, could be done to change the situation. In his 1973 book entitled, *Small is Beautiful: Economics as if People Mattered,* British economist E. F. Schumacher pointed to the nuclear industry as an example of technology run amuck. Many people agreed with Schumacher's argument that the sorry state of the environment resulted from society choosing technological options that gave immediate advantages without regard to the future of the human race.

As concern rose over dwindling natural resources, many people saw the materialism of modern society as the culprit. In order to keep the engine of capitalism running smoothly, business needs to keep producing, and consumers need to keep consuming. Advertising helps by convincing people that their happiness and well-being depends on them buying more, more, more. But environmentalists pointed out that the engine was being fueled by nonrenewable natural resources, and it was creating foul byproducts, namely pollution.

Environmentalists and others feared that the problems Schumacher described were intensified by the rapid growth of multinational corporations in the sixties and seventies. In 1973, for example, General Motors' annual sales were more than the gross national product of Switzerland, and by the same measure, Goodyear Tire was bigger than Saudi Arabia. Though leaders of the multinational corporations promoted the trend, claiming that it provided the means for the most efficient distribution of the world's resources, opponents saw in it many dangers.

For one thing, global corporations threatened to usurp the power of governments. As the former Under Secretary of State George Ball noted:

How can a national government make an economic plan with any confidence if a board of directors meeting 5,000 miles away can, by altering its pattern of purchasing and production, affect in a major way the country's economic life?

In addition, organized labor was threatened, for as corporate giants chose to relocate their plants to countries where labor was cheaper, thousands of workers lost their jobs. Still another fear was that global corporations led to a concentration of economic power as resources were directed to where they could get the most profit. In short, the rich got richer and the poor got poorer.

So, what was the solution? E. F. Schumacher and others argued for "decentralized economics" to promote local self-reliance. When corporations are locally owned and use local resources to produce products to be sold locally, Schumacher argued, they are more environmentally responsible. The problem of displaced workers is also relieved. Though many people agreed with Schumacher's ideas, others called his proposal an unrealistic, utopian dream. As the seventies came to a close, society's love/hate relationship with progress continued, and the question remained, could humankind learn to use technology responsibly, so that it really meant progress for all, or would it create more problems than it solved?

"The present consumer society is like a drug addict who, no matter how miserable he may feel, finds it extremely difficult to get off the hook."

E. F. Schumacher, economist

CHAPTER 9
A New President and a New Direction

The Ford Presidency

Ordinarily, an incoming president has eleven weeks between the election and inauguration to plan his agenda and recruit his staff. Gerald Ford did not have that luxury. Up until one week before Nixon's resignation, Ford had been defending the president. Obviously, he did not have much time to plan his own administration, though some plans were made without him. Ford's transition was especially difficult because staff members from the Nixon administration had to be kept on until Ford could find replacements. Power struggles between the Nixon holdovers and the Ford appointees made an already tense White House even more so.

On top of internal White House problems, Ford was faced with a troubling combination of high unemployment and rising inflation, an economic condition labeled "stagflation." In an effort to slow inflation, Ford was determined to cut federal spending, which led to many battles with Congress. During his short term, Ford handed down sixty-six vetoes, many of which were overridden. Ford also sought to involve American citizens in the fight against inflation, asking them to help the economy by cutting back on spending and saving more money. The White House launched a program called Whip Inflation Now, or WIN for short, sending out thou-

sands of WIN buttons to the public. Critics in the media called the program a simple-minded public relations campaign, however, and the WIN campaign was quietly abandoned.

But Ford's popularity rose again when he took forceful action in response to a crisis situation. In May of 1975, an American merchant ship named the *Mayaguez* was captured by Cambodian forces. It was just one month after the frantic evacuation of the U.S. embassy in Saigon, and Ford realized that the entire world was watching to see how he would respond to this threat to U.S. authority. Ford acted quickly, sending in the marines to rescue the ship and its thirty-nine crewmen, and ordering the bombardment of Cambodia as well. But, even before the marines arrived on the scene, the Cambodians had already decided to release the crew of the *Mayaguez*. When the American troops boarded the ship, they found it empty. But during the attack, forty-one Americans were killed and forty-nine were injured. It seemed a high price to pay, but the president and even the press lauded the *Mayaguez* mission as proof that the U.S. was not a helpless giant. The American public, for the most part, seemed eager to believe this good news after suffering through the debacle of Vietnam.

Despite the temporary rise in Ford's popularity, many Republicans feared he would be a weak presidential candidate in the 1976 election.

U. S. Marines raise the American flag aboard the Mayaguez *in May 1975, after recapturing the ship from Cambodian forces. Despite heavy casualties, many Americans were happy to see signs of decisive action from President Ford.*

POLITICS

For further information see primary source entries on pages

11: 1482-83; **12:** 1603-04, 1620-24, 1632-35, 1682-85, 1688-89, 1692-94, 1700-01, 1706-09, 1727-30

Handicapped by a lackluster speaking style, Ford was also plagued by an image problem that began when he slipped and fell as he descended the steps of an airplane. Thereafter the media highlighted every stumble and gaffe the president made, portraying him as a bumbler. In addition to his own party's misgivings and criticism from the press, Ford almost fell victim to a much more serious threat. In September of 1975, two attempts were made on the president's life. The first was by Lynette "Squeaky" Fromme, a follower of mass murderer Charles Manson, and the second by Sara Jane Moore, who was associated with the radical group that kidnapped heiress Patty Hearst. Tragically, violence seemed to be becoming a regular part of American politics. Still, even the threats to his life did not deter Ford from seeking election. Though he had not originally sought the presidency, he felt he needed four more years to carry out his agenda. But he was not the only man who longed to prove what he could accomplish in the White House.

Jimmy Who?

Jimmy Carter's rapid rise from obscurity to the presidency is one of the most remarkable stories in the history of U.S. politics. A born-again Christian, former peanut farmer, and one-term governor of Georgia, Carter was an unknown to most Americans when he first announced his candidacy in December of 1974. But what he lacked in prominence he made up for in determination. With no official duties to fulfill, Carter was able to campaign full-time, traveling all over the country to speak at small gatherings and shake hands at train stations and factories. Though he started out with few resources, he was supported by family members, friends, and volunteers who called themselves the "Peanut Brigade," who helped him wage a campaign in almost every primary. The tireless campaigning paid off when Carter won the first and most important Democratic state caucus in Iowa, making him a credible candidate. Carter was also well aware of the power of the media and did all he could to garner attention from the press, radio, and television. He made a point of becoming acquainted with powerful people in the media. The strategy proved highly effective, for when the media began focusing on him as the front-runner, Carter's campaign gained momentum.

Part of Carter's appeal to voters was his outsider status, which he made the most of. The Vietnam War and the Watergate scandal had left most Americans wary of anything or anyone associated with Washington. As Carter's pollster Patrick Cadell recalls, "Jimmy was a stranger in town. They had no reason to distrust him, and he didn't give them one." Carter chose to run a populist campaign, taking his appeal directly to the voters rather than working through the traditional Democratic party machinery. Refusing to be labeled conservative or liberal, he avoided getting too specific on the issues and focused instead on his own character. Carter promised time and again that as president, he would be honest and accountable to the people. After the trauma of Watergate, Carter's image as an ordinary person, his close ties to his family, and his unembarrassed discussions of his religious faith were a refreshing change.

Though Carter seemed unstoppable on his way to the Democratic nomination, his race against Ford was much closer. In the end, with only 54.4 percent of Americans voting, Carter won by a slim margin.

A New Style in the White House

As early as inauguration day, Carter proved that he intended to govern the nation with a completely different style than that of his predecessors. Instead of being driven in a limousine down the inaugural parade route to the White House, Carter and his family walked down Pennsylvania Avenue amidst the cheers of astonished crowds lining the street. As Carter recalled in his memoirs:

"Because of the heavy emphasis that was placed on Soviet-American competition, a dominant feature in our dealings with foreign countries became whether they espoused an anticommunist line. There were times when right-wing monarchs and military dictators were automatically immune from any criticism of their oppressive actions."

Jimmy Carter

The president and first lady break with tradition and walk along the inaugural parade route to the White House on January 20, 1977. The Carters brought an informal style to the White House, anxious to avoid the secrecy that had been the hallmark of the Nixon administration.

I wanted to provide a vivid demonstration of my confidence in the people as far as security was concerned, and I felt a simple walk would be a tangible indication of some reduction in the imperial status of the president and his family.

After the secrecy surrounding the Nixon administration, Carter felt it was important that he be perceived as a president of the people. Towards that goal, he put an end to much of the "pomp and circumstance" in the White House as he and his first lady, Rosalyn, introduced a more relaxed and informal style.

The Focus on Human Rights

Carter's emphasis on a more honest and open government was reflected in his foreign policy as well. During the 1976 campaign, Carter decried Kissinger's reliance on secret diplomacy and his philosophy on foreign affairs, which considered only national advancement. It wasn't just

Kissinger's style that Carter objected to, however, but also the general trend of a foreign policy driven entirely by the Cold War. By disregarding human rights abuses in foreign relations, Carter believed that the U.S. violated the very ideals on which the country was founded. With characteristic earnestness, Carter stated that the United Sates should "set a standard within the community of nations of courage, compassion, integrity, and dedication to basic human rights and freedoms." Carter hoped that by making human rights a cornerstone of his foreign policy, the U.S. could pressure other countries to stop abuses of their citizens.

Though the American public was generally in favor of the human rights policy, it proved to be difficult to carry out. Many countries objected to what they perceived as U.S. intervention in their internal affairs. Argentina, Brazil, El Salvador, and Guatemala rejected U.S. military aid after being criticized by the United States for human rights violations. The USSR also strongly opposed

Andrew Young.

After the death of Martin Luther King, Jr., his close friend and top aide, Andrew Young, realized that the civil rights movement had to enter a new phase. "There just comes a time when any movement has to come off the street and enter politics," said Young. In 1972, he was elected Representative of the Fifth Congressional District of Georgia, making him the first African-American voted into the House from the Deep South since 1898.

Once in Congress, Young developed a reputation as a liberal voter who pursued a path of quiet negotiation rather than confrontation over racial issues. "We have to find the kinds of programs that deal with the structural issues of poverty and unemployment by linking together the needs of black people and the needs of the rest of society," he said. Young easily won reelection in 1974 and again in 1976, gaining much respect and authority with each passing year.

As the 1976 presidential election drew near, candidate Jimmy Carter sought Young's advice and support, hoping that the congressman's approval would assure African-American voters that a southern white man could be trusted. Young's backing was indeed influential in Carter's win, and the new president acknowledged that Young was the only man to whom he was politically indebted.

Carter repaid that debt by appointing Young U.S. Ambassador to the United Nations, which he elevated to a cabinet post. But critics claimed Young was abandoning Georgia for a position that held no influence. Young was determined to make an impact at the UN, however, and it wasn't long before he did just that.

The new ambassador soon came under attack for making a number of controversial statements, some of which contradicted U.S. State Department policy. An outspoken critic of racism around the world, Young made several off-the-cuff comments that were quoted out of context, making for strident, inflammatory headlines. Though Young's reputation for speaking openly and honestly won him the trust of many Third World and African nations, conservatives in Congress began calling for his impeachment.

Carter supported Young through the storm of controversy, but the final straw came when Young held an unauthorized meeting with a member of the Palestinian Liberation Organization, which outraged America's Israeli allies. After being reprimanded for his actions, Young resigned from the post.

> *"We trust the shah to maintain stability in Iran, to continue with the democratic process."*
>
> Jimmy Carter, 1978

Carter's "personal pledge to promote human rights in the Soviet Union." Back home, critics attacked Carter for being naive and for jeopardizing important international relations. Carter was also criticized for being inconsistent in his standards. For example, despite the shah of Iran's "increasingly serious violations of human rights," Carter found that U.S. interests were so deeply intertwined with the shah's regime that he could not pull back U.S. support.

Carter's focus on human rights revealed a certain moral zeal and ambitiousness with which he also approached foreign policy. This same determination motivated him to attempt to resolve several difficult, ongoing problems. Carter hoped to follow through on what Nixon had begun by normalizing diplomatic relations between the United States and China, and he also hoped to agree on a SALT II treaty with the Soviet Union that would result in deep cuts in nuclear arsenals. Most of Carter's advisors agreed on the need to continue negotiations with the Communist superpowers, but the new president was also determined to resolve two rather messy, long-standing foreign relations problems that many of his advisors would have preferred he avoid.

The Panama Canal Treaty

In 1903, the United States signed a treaty with a French businessman representing the new Republic of Panama that gave the U.S. the right to build, operate, and defend a canal across the isthmus of Central America. In addition, the U.S. was granted "all the rights, power and authority" to control a ten-mile-wide strip of land known as the Canal Zone that divided Panama in two. Since its inception, the treaty had been a source of great bitterness to Panamanians, and tensions in the area frequently erupted in violence. In 1964, twenty-nine people were killed in anti-American demonstrations in Panama. In response, the Johnson administration agreed to renegotiate the canal treaties. But Johnson, Nixon, and Ford were all thwarted in their efforts to renegotiate by critics in the U.S. and in Congress especially, who believed that giving up the canal would pose a security risk. The issue was also dear to patriots, for as one of the world's greatest engineering achievements, the canal was a source of national pride.

Several of Jimmy Carter's advisors, including his wife Rosalyn, urged him to put off the canal problem, deeming it too politically risky. But Carter was determined to make it a priority. He wrote in his memoirs:

I was convinced that we needed to correct an injustice. Our failure to take action after years of promises under five previous presidents had created something of a diplomatic cancer, which was poisoning our relations with Panama.

The Panama Canal was a great engineering achievement when it was built at the beginning of the century. Americans were proud of it and felt it belonged to them forever. President Carter was prepared to give the canal back to Panama, hoping to foster better relations with Latin American countries.

> "When it comes to the canal, we built it, we paid for it, it's ours ... we are going to keep it."
>
> Ronald Reagan, in the 1976 primaries

Intelligence sources indicated that disgruntled Panamanians might even sabotage or blow up the canal if the U.S. did not agree to a new arrangement. In fact, not only Panama but much of Latin America was growing impatient with the imperial attitude of the U.S. toward the canal. Though polls indicated that most Americans were against ever giving up control of the canal, Carter believed that if he presented the facts clearly, he could convince the public and Congress of the need to change the treaty and thereby remove the wedge between the U.S. and Latin America.

Carter negotiated a treaty that gave the Canal Zone back to Panama while guaranteeing the United States the right to continue to operate and defend the canal until the year 2000. He then set out on an intense lobbying campaign to convince Congress to ratify the treaty. One by one, he worked on the senators, urging them to make what was for many a politically unpopular decision. When the treaty was finally ratified in April of 1978, Carter remembers that he was both exhausted and exhilarated. But five months later he would embark on an even more arduous mission.

The Camp David Accord

Shortly after taking office, Carter made it clear that he intended to work toward achieving a settlement in the Middle East. The 1973 Yom Kippur War between Israel and the Arab nations that led to the oil embargo had left the region extremely volatile, with sporadic violence threatening once again to escalate into war. Most of Carter's advisors urged him to stay out of the Middle East conflict, believing that the chances for success in that strife-ridden region were too slim. But Carter felt differently. "I could see growing threats to the United States in the Middle East," he wrote, "and was willing to make another try, perhaps overly confident that I could now find answers that had eluded so many others."

At first, the Carter administration tried to help the rival countries reach a settlement through the protection of the United Nations and other diplomatic channels. When it became clear that Egypt and Israel would not be able to reach an agreement on their own, the United States attempted to draft a plan that would be agreeable to both. But negotiations reached a standstill, and Carter began seeking other paths to a resolution. Believing a bold move was called for, Carter suggested that he personally mediate negotiations between Israeli Prime Minister Menachem Begin and Egyptian President Anwar el-Sadat. Carter believed that within the peaceful confines of the presidential retreat known as Camp David, the three leaders might be able to reach an agreement. Many of Carter's advisors were against the idea, for if the meeting failed, Carter would be held responsible. Democratic congressmen and party officials also warned Carter that his Middle East efforts were damaging political relations with the American Jewish community, which was concerned about Israel's security. But Carter was determined to go all out for peace.

The three leaders originally agreed to stay at Camp David for at least three days, and if negotiations were going well, for up to one week. In the end, they spent thirteen intense, grueling, and often discouraging days at the retreat. While Carter and Sadat had developed a close and trusting friendship, Begin and Sadat disliked each other, and each threatened to leave Camp David when it appeared an agreement was impossible. Though negotiations seemed to be on the brink of collapsing, Carter refused to give up. Having studied the situation intensely, he relied on all of his intelligence and his homework as he tirelessly pursued an agreement between the two men. Carter made personal appeals to their morals and their hopes for peace, trying to make each see things from the other country's side. Sadat's trust in Carter was critical, for it allowed Carter to work out an agreement with Begin.

Finally, on September 17, 1978, the three leaders emerged from Camp David to make the dramatic announcement that they had reached an accord. Two treaties were signed that day. The first, entitled "Framework for Peace in the Middle East," called for more negotiations to determine the future of the West Bank, an Israeli-ruled area. The agreement represented a major con-cession by Sadat, for Arab countries wanted a Palestinian state to be created in the area, but Begin did agree to "recognize the legitimate rights of Palestinians." The second treaty, entitled "Framework for the Conclusion of a Peace Treaty Between Egypt and Israel" called for Israel to withdraw from the Sinai peninsula, an area it had captured from Egypt in the 1967 Six-Day War. Both countries also agreed to move toward normal diplomatic relations. Acknowledging Carter's crucial role as mediator, Begin said the agreement should be called the "Jimmy Carter Accords," and joked that "he worked harder than our forefathers did in Egypt building the pyramids."

Despite the goodwill created by the Camp David accord, once the two leaders returned to their countries and were faced with the tensions there, the agreement threatened to fall apart. In 1979, Carter made a personal trip to the Middle East to restore the agreement. The Camp David accord is considered one of Jimmy Carter's greatest achievements as president.

Egyptian President Anwar el-Sadat, President Jimmy Carter, and Israeli Prime Minister Menachem Begin sign the Middle East Peace Treaty. It was risky for Carter to get involved in the negotiations, as failure would have reflected badly on him. After two weeks of tense discussions and delicate maneuvering, the three men constructed the Camp David Accord.

CHAPTER 10
A Crisis of Confidence

An Outsider in Charge

On the campaign trail, Jimmy Carter's image as an outsider who hadn't been tainted by Washington appealed to millions of voters who had become jaded by Vietnam and Watergate. Carter's anti-Washington message was genuine and not merely a campaign ploy, for he was innately opposed to the excessive bureaucracy and "horse-trading" style of politics Washington is known for. The irony is that the outsider status that helped Carter win the election became a liability once he became president.

Washington insiders were instantly skeptical of the born-again Baptist from the Deep South coming in to take over. Cartoons portrayed Carter and his Georgian aides as barefoot country bumpkins, arriving at the White House in ragged overalls with bewildered expressions on their faces. In addition, much of Carter's staff was more youthful than Washington was used to, and this generation gap led to some image problems for the new administration. When two of Carter's top aides, Hamilton Jordan and Jody Powell, posed for the cover of *Rolling Stone* magazine as Butch Cassidy and the Sundance Kid, critics accused them of not taking their jobs seriously enough.

But more importantly, the Carter administration lacked a practical vision of how to conduct relations with Congress. Despite Carter's distaste for a "you-scratch-my-back-and-I'll-scratch-yours" style of government, that was how Congress functioned. In the first two years of his presidency especially, Carter was uninterested in compromising with Congress. He was only concerned with putting forth the best policies. For example, during the first weeks of his administration, Carter recommended eliminating funding for nineteen water projects (involving dam constructions, etc.) on the grounds that they were damaging to the environment and a waste of taxpayer's money. However, some of the regions affected by the proposed cuts were represented by powerful members of Congress. They considered the water projects a "political plum," for not only would they provide jobs for their constituents, but they would also prove that the representatives had some clout in Washington. Though Carter managed to eliminate nine of the water projects, he created a rift between himself and the congressional leadership in the process.

Of course, Carter's outsider message was not the only thing that propelled him to office. It was also his idealism, his ambitious "can-do" attitude that attracted voters. But once Carter arrived in Washington, his ambitious agenda began to create difficulties with Congress. One week after assuming the presidency, Carter wrote in his diary, "Everybody has warned me not to take on too many projects so early in the administration, but it's almost impossible for me to delay something that I see needs to be

Rosalyn Carter.

"The President of the United States cares what I think," said Rosalyn Carter. "I find myself in the eye of history. I have influence. And I know it." In fact, Jimmy Carter referred to Rosalyn as "a very equal partner," and she was considered the most influential first lady since Eleanor Roosevelt.

As the wife of the president, Rosalyn projected a confident, self-assured image, but she had not always seemed so. When her husband ran for governor of Georgia in 1970, Rosalyn struggled to overcome her extreme shyness and fear of public speaking in order to help him in his campaign. As the governor's wife, she grew more comfortable giving speeches and with political life.

When Jimmy decided to run for president, Rosalyn helped convince him to run in every primary and then spent almost two years crisscrossing the country without him, spreading the candidate's message to anyone who would listen. Her gentle southern charm, combined with her strong support for "my Jimmy," as she called him, led some reporters to dub her the "Steel Magnolia." But Rosalyn rejected that name, pointing out that she did not just "stand by her man" but pursued her own independent interests as well. As first lady, she actively promoted mental health programs and the needs of the elderly and was an outspoken supporter of the Equal Rights Amendment. She also had little patience for reporters who paid more attention to how she dressed or what she served in the White House than to her favorite causes.

Rosalyn regularly attended cabinet meetings, which some observers objected to, and often had a strong input in her husband's deliberations. "Her judgment is superb," one aide to the president reported, especially in matters of political strategy and in choosing appointees. Jimmy Carter was so confident of Rosalyn's abilities that he often sent her as an ambassador on important missions. She also testified before congressional committees as the honorary chairperson of the President's Commission on Mental Health, and when the Panama Canal treaties were in trouble, she embarked on an intensive lobbying campaign to shore up support. In an article entitled "Mrs. President," *Newsweek* magazine summed up Rosalyn Carter's influence: "She is, in short, a one-woman kitchen cabinet, Carter's most trusted, senior hand."

Rosalyn Carter visits a refugee camp in Thailand in 1979.

done." During the first months of his administration, President Carter proposed comprehensive policies for, among other things, welfare reform, government reorganization, an energy program, and an anti-inflation program. Congress complained they were being swamped by proposals without any clear guidance from the White House as to what should be given priority. Cabinet secretaries and White House staff members were spread so thin that they often couldn't do an effective job of selling the programs, and Carter himself was uncomfortable using the persuasive powers of the presidency to get his proposals through. As he acknowledged in an interview, "I've never had the inclination nor the knowledge about the process to twist arms or force people to vote different from what they thought."

The Problem with Conservative Liberalism

As a presidential candidate, Jimmy Carter had frustrated many reporters by his refusal to be pinned down as either a liberal or a conservative. On the one hand, he was the only Democratic candidate to promise, or even mention, a balanced budget and fiscal responsibility, which clearly made him the most conservative choice. But, as a deeply religious man who witnessed poverty and prejudice growing up in the rural South, Carter was also a sincere advocate of the poor and of civil rights. Carter's activist stance on social issues cast him as a liberal in many people's minds.

Once he was in the White House, Carter's combination of liberal goals and fiscal conservatism often resulted in problems on Capitol Hill. By attempting a centrist approach, Carter angered Republicans, who labeled his social programs too liberal, and Democrats, who deemed his budgets too conservative. Congressional liberals such as House Speaker Tip O'Neill and Congresswoman Shirley Chisholm accused him of neglecting social programs in his quest to balance the budget. But Carter insisted on both "prudence and boldness." As his aide Stuart Eizenstat remembers:

One always knew that he [Carter] wanted to spend as little money as possible and yet at the same time he wanted welfare reform . . . national health insurance . . . an urban policy . . . job training programs.

These seemingly contradictory goals led to the criticism that Carter's administration was unrealistic and even naive.

The Energy Crisis

In addition to its internal problems, the Carter administration was faced with a growing problem that its two Republican predecessors had been unable to solve. With domestic oil production in decline, the 1973 Arab oil embargo had shown the United States just how dangerous its increasing dependence on costly foreign oil could be. Available supplies of oil and natural gas continued to diminish as the demand for energy became ever greater. Carter had promised in his election campaign to create an energy program to deal with the issue.

Shortly after Carter was sworn in, he was faced with a crisis. The Northeast suffered from a combination of severe winter weather and a natural gas shortage, forcing schools and factories to close temporarily. The president proposed an Emergency Natural Gas Act to create a more equitable distribution of natural gas throughout the country, and Congress passed the bill within one week. Seizing on the drama of the moment, Carter gave his first televised "fireside chat" to announce to the American people that he intended to submit a comprehensive energy plan to Congress. Two months later, just before Carter presented his plan to Congress, he appeared on television once again to outline what was at stake:

The energy crisis has not yet overwhelmed us, but it will if we do not act quickly. . . . This difficult effort will be the "moral equivalent of war," except that we will be uniting our efforts to build and not to destroy.

Arab oil ministers at an OPEC conference in Abu Dhabi, in the United Arab Emirates, meeting in December 1978 to set a new price for crude oil. Reduced Arab oil production in 1979 led to another shortage for motorists and made the American economic recession worse.

The plan included a number of incentives to promote energy conservation, increase fuel production in the United States, and develop alternative energy sources. Demonstrating a commitment to practice what he preached, Carter ordered the heat in the White House to be kept at fifty-five degrees at night and sixty-five during the day, a sacrifice that induced Rosalyn Carter to wear long underwear to keep warm.

Carter's energy strategy passed through the House quickly enough, but conflict in the Senate delayed passage of the bill for eighteen months. When it finally was signed into law in November of 1978, it was a weaker bill than Carter had envisioned, but the National Energy Act still represented an important achievement.

The United States' energy prob-lems were far from over, however. In 1979, OPEC once again asserted its power by holding down oil production, which caused prices to rise by more than 50 percent in six months. Economies all over the world were rocked by the "second oil shock." In the U.S., motorists began panic-buying, creating hours-long lines at gas stations throughout the country. Americans were frustrated and discouraged by the shortage, and polls showed they held the president partly responsible. His popularity plunged to a new low.

In July, Carter retreated to Camp David for ten days to reassess his administration with help from a variety of experts and advisors. When he emerged, he gave a dramatic televised address in which he talked of a severe "threat" facing the nation:

ECONOMY

For further information see primary source entries on pages

11: 1526-28, 1537-39, 1550-53; **12:** 1611-12, 1680-81, 1702-03, 1722-26

This diagram shows that an item that cost $100 in 1967 rose in price until it cost $272 in 1981. This was the result of steadily rising inflation, which successive governments were unable to control.

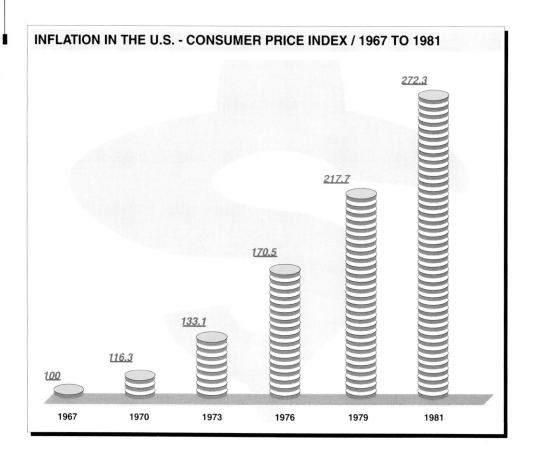

INFLATION IN THE U.S. - CONSUMER PRICE INDEX / 1967 TO 1981

- 272.3 — 1981
- 217.7 — 1979
- 170.5 — 1976
- 133.1 — 1973
- 116.3 — 1970
- 100 — 1967

It is a crisis of confidence. It is a crisis that strikes at the very heart and soul and spirit of our national will. We can see this crisis in the growing doubt about the meaning of our own lives and in the loss of a unity of purpose for our nation. The erosion of our confidence in the future is threatening to destroy the social and the political fabric of America.

Carter called on Americans to work together to restore faith in their country and realize its potential. Though initial reaction to the speech was positive, the president's approval rating fell again after he demanded letters of resignation from all of his Cabinet and accepted five of them. Carter seemed to be flailing around in search of direction, an image which made Americans even less confident in him.

The Economic Quagmire

One of the most difficult problems Carter faced was how to fulfill his campaign promise to move the economy out of recession without worsening inflation. The solution remained elusive, for throughout Jimmy Carter's four years as president, the inflation rate steadily climbed. Some blamed the expensive federal entitlement programs passed in the sixties. Others pointed to a variety of factors, including costly environmental regulations and the falling value of the dollar on international markets. Everyone agreed that the OPEC oil shock had a disastrous effect. Though some of the factors were out of Carter's control, as long

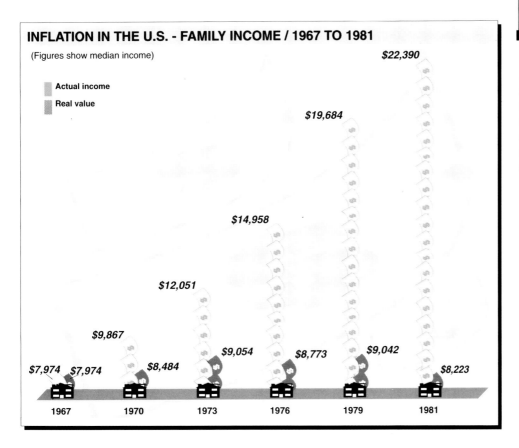

INFLATION IN THE U.S. - FAMILY INCOME / 1967 TO 1981

(Figures show median income)

■ Actual income
■ Real value

$7,974 $7,974 — 1967
$9,867 $8,484 — 1970
$12,051 $9,054 — 1973
$14,958 $8,773 — 1976
$19,684 $9,042 — 1979
$22,390 $8,223 — 1981

Incomes increased greatly between 1967 and 1981, but the value of that money remained much the same throughout the period because inflation rose so dramatically.

as he was in the White House, he would incur a large portion of the blame for inflation. By 1979, inflation was at 11.3 percent and rising.

The high cost of living was not the only problem with inflation. As the prices of houses soared, property taxes rose at a corresponding rate. By 1978, many taxpayers in California had had enough. They voted in favor of Proposition 13, an amendment to their state constitution that cut seven billion dollars in property taxes. The referendum results sent a strong message to politicians everywhere, and other states began looking into taking the same action.

In addition to the sad state of the economy and the energy crisis, Carter faced a number of foreign policy crises as he prepared to run for reelection in 1980. The most dramatic crisis was one that seemed an almost inevitable outcome of a disturbing trend.

The Rise of Terrorism

Throughout the seventies, the world saw a steady rise in terrorism, defined by writer Thomas Snitch as the "systematic attempt to induce fear and anxiety among people expressly for some political purpose." The early seventies brought a wave of airplane hijackings, and in 1976 there were a record number of bombings and assassinations.

Nearly every part of the world seemed to have its terrorist organizations. In the Middle East, Palestinian terrorists set off bombs and carried out assassinations. Britain was troubled by the Irish Republican Army, and Italy was afflicted with the Red Brigades. In the U.S., the Weather Underground was responsible for at least twenty bombings between 1970 and 1975.

According to Thomas Snitch, television was an "essential tool" for terrorists, for it allowed them to effectively spread their message to a wide audience. Governments were then faced with the very difficult question of how to react while that large audience was watching. If the governments overreacted with a tough crackdown, the public might feel sympathetic towards the terrorists. But if the governments hesitated or didn't react strongly enough, they would appear weak and ineffectual.

Measures were taken to prevent and discourage terrorism. Airports tightened security, installing baggage x-ray machines. Guards were added around government buildings. In 1978, the seven leading industrial nations agreed to halt all flights to and from any country giving sanctuary to hijackers, and they agreed to share information on terrorists.

There was also a call for all of the nations to agree never to bargain with terrorists, which was the U.S. policy. While in theory a "no bargain" convention seemed likely to discourage terrorism, it could in reality lead to a political and moral dilemma. Was the U.S. government really willing to stand up to public reaction if its citizens were killed by terrorists after the U.S. refused to negotiate? Jimmy Carter would soon gain first-hand experience in dealing with the thorny issue of terrorism.

The Iranian Revolution

During the seventies, a revival of Islamic fundamentalism was underway in several Muslim countries. Many of them had been under colonial rule in the early part of the century, and now, with independence and the wealth from oil profits, they became confident enough to reject the influence of Western culture and reassert

Ayatollah Khomeini waves to followers after returning to Iran from exile in 1979. Islamic fundamentalism was revived in many Muslim countries, and Western culture and domination were rejected. This movement was particularly strong in Iran, where the shah had been in power for thirty-eight years, aided by the West. U.S. support for his corrupt regime fostered intense hatred among Iranian fundamentalists for all things American.

their Islamic traditions. The revival of Islamic fundamentalism created serious problems for the shah of Iran, whose regime had received billions of dollars from the United States in return for protection of U.S. oil interests there. Followers of the exiled Muslim leader Ayatollah Khomeini rebelled against the U.S. embassy in Tehran, taking sixty-three Americans hostage and demanding that the shah be returned to Iran to stand trial.

Scenes of blindfolded Americans being paraded in front of cameras horrified the public back home, and the hostage story became a national

In November 1979, Iranian students seized the U.S. Embassy in Tehran, taking sixty-three American hostages and demanding the return of the Shah for trial. Once again, Americans saw their country humiliated on their television screens.

the shah's corrupt, pro-Western regime, whose secret police were increasingly notorious for torture.

In January of 1979, the shah fled, bringing an end to his thirty-eight-year reign. Shortly thereafter, the Ayatollah returned to Iran and seized the reins of power in a fundamentalist revolution. Ayatollah Khomeini condemned the U.S. for its support of the shah, denouncing it as a "foreign devil" and encouraging his followers to take to the streets in virulent anti-U.S. demonstrations. After the shah was allowed into the U.S. for medical treatment, the hatred for the U.S. reached fever pitch. In November of 1979, student revolutionaries seized

crisis that dominated television news. ABC TV began a program hosted by journalist Ted Koppel, which provided updates on the situation every weeknight at 11:30 Eastern Time. Originally called *America Held Hostage*, the program evolved into *Nightline*. Carter was deeply grieved by the crisis. He met with family members of the hostages and searched desperately for a solution to the dilemma. The president vowed to stay near Washington and said he would not make any political appearances until the hostages were released, despite the onset of campaign season. As is usual in crisis situations, the public rallied behind the president. Some critics accused Carter of exploiting

POLITICS

For further information see primary source entries on pages

11: 1482-83; **12:** 1603-04, 1620-24, 1632-35, 1682-85, 1688-89, 1692-94, 1700-01, 1706-09, 1727-30

the hostage crisis by waging what was called "the Rose Garden strategy" in an effort to dodge the more controversial campaign issues and appear more presidential than his opponents.

A Rift with the Soviets

The Iranian revolution led to another foreign policy crisis. In December of 1979, the Soviet Union invaded Afghanistan, fearing that the Islamic revolution would spread to the neighboring Marxist country. The surprising resurgence of Soviet aggression instantly jeopardized the policy of détente. Not only would a Soviet takeover of Afghanistan change the balance of power in that region, it could also threaten important oil fields in the Persian Gulf area. Critics held Carter partly responsible for his comparatively lenient attitude toward communism, but Carter was determined not to be lenient in his response to the invasion.

The president immediately sent Brezhnev a message on the "hot line," warning him that if Soviet troops were not withdrawn, the invasion would "jeopardize the course of United States-Soviet relations throughout the world." When the Soviets continued to send forces into Afghanistan, Carter issued a grain embargo, immediately canceling delivery of seventeen million tons of grain that the Soviets had purchased. In addition, Carter made a highly controversial decision to boycott the 1980 summer Olympics, which were to be held in Moscow. Though many athletes who had spent years training for the event were crushed and critics attacked Carter for politicizing the Olympics, Carter felt that it was "unconscionable to be guests of the Soviets while they were involved in a bloody suppression of the people of Afghanistan."

To Jimmy Carter, one of the most painful results of the Soviet invasion was that it put a halt to ratification of the

Soviet army reinforcements arrive in Kabul, during their invasion of Afghanistan in January 1980. The Soviet Union took this action to support Afghanistan's troubled Marxist regime.

SALT II treaty, an agreement to limit long-range nuclear weapons. Years of arduous effort had gone into negotiating the treaty, and only six months before the invasion, Carter and Brezhnev had hammered out their final differences in the agreement. The Senate was in the process of debating ratification when the Soviets invaded Afghanistan. Realizing that the treaty clearly stood no chance in the current atmosphere, Carter withdrew it from consideration. Though the agreement provided the foundation for later negotiations, Carter regarded the failure to ratify SALT II and to negotiate stronger arms control as "the most profound disappointment of my presidency."

Trouble in Central America

Yet another foreign policy crisis faced Carter in 1979. In Nicaragua, Communist Sandinistas (named after a murdered leftist leader named Augusto Sandino) overthrew the government of Anastasio Somoza. Somoza's family had ruled Nicaragua since 1933, when his father gained power with the help of U.S. backing.

Carter came under criticism for not taking a hard line against the Communists and for not supporting Somoza. But Carter was offended by the Somoza regime's record of human rights violations. He hoped the Sandinistas would live up to their promise to establish a democracy, but by 1980, Carter realized this was unlikely.

Critics called Carter naive for trusting the Sandinistas, but Carter later wrote that he was trying to prevent Nicaragua from turning into another Cuba, cut off from the United States and closely allied with the Soviet Union.

Nicaragua was not the only hot spot in Latin America. In 1979, civil war broke out in El Salvador between the ruling military junta and left-wing revolutionaries. Though Carter was deeply disturbed by the stories of government-backed death squads, he nonetheless increased the amount of military aid to the El Salvadorean junta.

Growing Frustration

As the seventies drew to a close, Americans were faced with crises abroad and uncertainty at home: the hostages in Iran, the Soviets in Afghanistan, bloody civil wars in Central America, and rising inflation rates in the U.S. The "crisis of confidence" President Carter identified in July 1979 had only grown worse since then, and Americans were becoming increasingly frustrated. As the 1980 presidential campaign began, many voters were eager for an alternative to the government of the last four years.

Communist Sandinista rebels celebrate in front of the national palace in Managua, Nicaragua, in July 1979. They had overthrown the corrupt Somoza government that had controlled the country for forty-six years. Many Americans felt that President Carter should have supported the government to prevent a Communist takeover.

CHAPTER 11
The End of an Era and the Shape of Things to Come

A Turning Point

During the seventies, the United States underwent something of an identity crisis. Since its inception, the U.S. had been perceived as a nation full of hope and promise. After World War II, the United States emerged as the leader of the free world, and its potential appeared limitless. Rapid progress in science and technology swelled expectations, and the economy blossomed as well, creating the wealthiest society in the world. But then a number of unforeseen circumstances, both at home and abroad, combined during the seventies to lead some Americans to wonder whether their country's glory days were in the past.

The American Dream in Doubt

As the writer Nicholas Lemann observed:

The nearly universal assumption in the post-World War II United States was that children would do better than their parents. Upward mobility wasn't just a characteristic of the national culture; it was the defining characteristic.

During the seventies, however, the steady climb to ever more prosperity staggered when the economy took a turn for the worse. The decade brought the highest unemployment rate since 1941 and the deepest drop in industrial production since 1937. As inflation rates soared, the value of the dollar descended to new postwar lows, and suddenly many Americans doubted their ability to provide a better life for their children — a crucial part of the American dream.

Another component of the American dream is the belief that, through hard work and dedication, anyone can become a success in the United States. But as the civil rights movement and the women's movement stressed, African-Americans, other minorities, and women often faced formidable obstacles to success that white males did not. By raising the nation's consciousness, these movements successfully corrected many institutional inequalities, and during the seventies, blacks and women began taking advantage of the new opportunities that became available to them. But, at the same time, some people saw a disturbing trend developing. Increasingly, special interest groups were making demands on government without concern for, as Nicholas Lemann puts it, "the general good." In other words, American society seemed to be growing more and more fragmented, with each group looking out only for its own interests.

The American family was also fragmenting, as divorce statistics clearly proved. The old ideal of the traditional family, in which father worked, mother stayed home, and marriage meant forever, was losing ground. In a 1975 article titled "The American Family: Can It Survive Today's Shocks?" *U.S. News & World Report* noted that:

Marriage bonds are loosening under the strains of broad social and economic shifts in the nation at large — among them the quest of women for equality in the home and "fulfillment" in outside careers.

In addition, the forces that traditionally held marriages together, such as religion and social mores that frowned on divorce, were weakening at the same time that other outside forces were growing more influential. Dr. Richard A. Gardner, author of *The Boys and Girls Book About Divorce* observed:

The mass media constantly bombard us with images of jet setters and other ways of making individuals feel they're missing out on the good things of life. Because families no longer are wrapped up in survival and care of the children, they succumb more easily to distractions that could contribute to disruption.

The social environment of the "Me Decade" allowed for more personal freedom than ever before, but as the seventies progressed, Americans became more aware of the price of that freedom. Some analysts believe that this explains in part why *Roots* was such a tremendously popular television program, because its emphasis on the importance of family and heritage touched a nerve in a society whose family unit was undergoing such serious erosion. Though the

author of *Roots*, Alex Haley, took great pride in his family's genealogy, he knew firsthand the stresses facing the modern family, for he was divorced twice and had little contact with his children. As Richard M. Levine wrote in 1978, "Clearly, in Alex Haley, television has finally found a man whose insatiable nostalgia for the vanishing dream of the American family matches its own."

A Weakened World Leader

By the end of the seventies, many Americans were also nostalgic for a time when their country was at the pinnacle of power, the unquestioned leader of the free world. When the decade began, the antiwar movement was at a fevered pitch, and President Nixon was promising peace with honor in Vietnam. Though Nixon pledged to withdraw American troops, he and Kissinger still held out hope that North Vietnam could be beaten back and South Vietnam propped up enough for the U.S. to credibly declare victory and leave. But the sight on national TV news of Americans scrambling into helicopters in April 1975 as Saigon fell to the Communists made it impossible for even the most die-hard patriot to believe that the war had been won. Though an overwhelming majority of Americans had wanted out of the war, that didn't make the damage to their country's image any easier to accept. The guiding principle of American foreign policy ever since World War II had been to stop the spread of communism, but now, in Southeast Asia, the U.S. had failed.

What's more, the war in Vietnam

"The craze for genealogy ... is connected with the epidemic for divorce .... If we can't figure out who our living relatives are, then maybe we'll have more luck with the dead ones."

Jane Howard, *Families*

had deeply and bitterly divided Americans, and that division led to the most shocking repercussion of all — the fall of President Nixon. In his attempts to control press leaks that hampered his efforts in Vietnam, which in many ways would have more lasting consequences — the OPEC oil embargo. Not only did the oil embargo (and the second oil shock of 1979) wreak havoc on the world economy, but, as Lemann observes,

Americans are evacuated from Saigon by helicopter as the North Vietnamese prepare to overrun the city. Such images emphasized the fact that the Vietnam War had been a national disaster and a humiliation, damaging U.S. prestige around the world.

> *"The chief lesson of Watergate [is that the] stability of the American political system is profound .... The president of the republic was forced from office, and as a result nothing happened .... The tanks didn't roll, the junta delivered no communiques from the Pentagon, not even a drunk Republican took to the streets."*
>
> Tom Wolfe

Nixon laid the foundation for the Watergate scandal. Though the scandal came as a stunning blow to a nation trying to heal after the Vietnam War, some commentators found a silver lining in the dark cloud of Watergate, for the system of democracy had survived intact. However, the public's trust in their government had been most seriously violated.

While Americans were preoccupied with the Watergate hearings, another important event occurred

"It demonstrated that America could now be 'pushed around' by countries most of us had always thought of as minor powers." U.S dependence on foreign oil remained a stubborn problem that would affect foreign policy in the next decade and beyond. But an even more immediate and graphic demonstration of Americans being "pushed around" was the hostage crisis in Iran. The Soviet invasion of Afghanistan that same year added to feelings of frustration and anger over the apparent impotence of the U.S.

The trans-Alaska Pipeline System opened in 1977 to bring two million barrels of oil a day from Prudhoe Bay in Alaska south to the port of Valdez, seen here, in Prince William Sound. The eight hundred-mile long pipeline crosses hundreds of rivers and is held up by seventy-eight thousand supports. Prudhoe is the largest oil field in North America, and its opening allowed the U.S. to reduce its oil imports from the Middle East.

Frustration and the 1980 Elections

As president of the United States, Jimmy Carter was the recipient of much of that anger and frustration. Carter's 1979 televised address accurately described the crisis of confidence gripping the nation, but it did nothing to help resolve that crisis. According to writer Jules Witcover, "The consensus analysis was that Carter was trying to shift the blame for his failures onto the people, and it did not sit at all well with them." The people were looking for someone to lead them out of the crisis, but for a combination of reasons, including administrative ineptitude and external events, Carter proved unable to provide that leadership.

Carter's bid for reelection thus promised to be a rocky road. It was made even rockier after the Federal Reserve Board announced it was imposing stringent monetary controls in an attempt to curb inflation, causing interest rates to go through the roof. Then, in April of 1980, Carter authorized a mission to rescue the American hostages in Iran, but the attempt ended in disaster. Due to mechanical difficulties, the mission had to be aborted. As the transport planes and helicopters prepared to retreat, a helicopter collided with one of the transports, and eight men were killed. There appeared to be no sign of hope for the release of the hostages.

Lured by polls that showed Jimmy Carter's popularity ratings as low as 29 percent, Senator Edward Kennedy decided to challenge the incumbent for the Democratic nomination. An old-line liberal, Kennedy accused Carter of abandoning the traditional role of the Democratic party by cutting social programs while increasing defense spending. The message had a limited appeal, however, for as Proposition 13 proved, a growing number of Americans were revolting against higher taxes and the expensive welfare programs they believed were largely responsible. Kennedy was also hampered by a surprisingly weak campaigning style. After being unable to come up with a convincing answer to television reporter Roger Mudd's question, "Why do you want to be president?" Kennedy's standing in the polls began faltering. He eventually dropped out of the campaign, but not before inflicting considerable damage on the already beleaguered Carter.

Ronald Reagan and the Image of Strength

While Carter was busy fighting off Edward Kennedy, the candidate who would emerge as a more serious challenger was quickly pulling ahead in the Republican primary campaign — Ronald Reagan, the former governor of California. At first, Carter's campaign people looked on Reagan as the easiest Republican to beat. They believed he was too old and too conservative to win. They also recalled the crackpot economic ideas that Reagan proposed in his 1976 campaign for president, such as a plan to invest social security funds in the stock market. Despite such controversial proposals, Reagan had created some excitement in 1976, especially among conservatives, a group that now included a growing number of Americans. In that election, Reagan attacked détente as a flawed policy and vowed that if elected, he would never "give away" the Panama Canal. Ultimately, Reagan lost to the more moderate Ford.

But, by 1979, with the Soviets in Afghanistan and the hostages in Iran, Reagan's tough talk had a strong appeal. The nation's worsening economic problems also worked to the benefit of his campaign. Reagan had been an early supporter of Proposition 13 in California, and he easily tapped into the outrage many taxpayers were feeling. In his acceptance speech at the Republican National Convention in July of 1980, Reagan summed up the mood of frustration and dissatisfaction in the country:

Can you look at the record of this administration and say, "Well done?" Can anyone compare the state of our economy when the Carter administration took office with where we are today and say, "Keep up the good work?" Can you look at our reduced standing in the world today and say, "Let's have four more years of this?"

The audience roared back with a resounding "No!"

Reagan also had the advantage of his acting experience. In the television age, style is often more important than substance, and the tall, presidential looking Reagan skillfully projected an image of strength to a public that was hungry for a strong leader. While Jimmy Carter was calling on Americans to sacrifice and work together to heal their nation, Reagan refused to accept what he said was the Democratic party's belief that :

The United States has had its days in the sun, that our nation has passed its zenith. . . . that the future will be one of sacrifice and few opportunities. My fellow citizens, I utterly reject that view.

Eager for a new direction and a return to strength, voters cast their ballots for Reagan, and Americans bid good riddance to the seventies. But

"For the average American, the message is clear. Liberalism is no longer the answer. It is the problem."

Ronald Reagan

(Opposite) Ronald Reagan campaigns for the presidency in his home town of Tampico, Illinois. His acting experience gave him confidence, and his strong image and tough talk appealed to a public weary of the Carter administration.

though the decade had come to a close, it left behind a lasting legacy: the Vietnam syndrome; a lingering distrust of government resulting from Watergate; the dangers of depending on foreign oil — all these would have long-lasting effects on the United States for years to come.

KEY DATES

1970

Feminists commemorate the fiftieth anniversary of the Nineteenth Amendment with strikes and mass marches demanding equality.

Radical groups are involved in a number of bombings around the country.

Rock stars Janis Joplin and Jimi Hendrix are killed by drug overdose, both at the age of twenty-seven.

April 22 — The first Earth Day is celebrated.

April 30 — President Nixon announces that U.S. soldiers and South Vietnamese troops have entered Cambodia.

May 4 — Four Kent State students are killed by National Guardsmen during antiwar demonstrations.

1971

Daniel Ellsberg leaks the *Pentagon Papers* to the press.

Lieutenant William Calley, Jr., is convicted for his role in the My Lai massacre of Vietnamese civilians.

"All in the Family" makes its television debut, featuring the bigoted Archie Bunker.

May 1 — Massive antiwar marches in Washington result in a record 13,400 arrests.

1972

February 21-29 — President Nixon visits China, ending two decades of hostility.

May 15 — Presidential candidate George Wallace is paralyzed in an assassination attempt.

May 22-29 — Nixon becomes the first U.S. president to visit Moscow. The Strategic Arms Limitation Treaty (SALT I) is signed.

June 17 — Five men are arrested for breaking into the Democratic National Headquarters in the Watergate building.

September 5-6 — Seventeen people are killed after Palestinian terrorists seize Israeli athletes at the Munich Olympics.

November 7 — President Richard Nixon and Vice President Spiro Agnew win reelection in a landslide victory over Senator George McGovern and his running mate, R. Sargent Shriver.

December 7 — *Apollo 17,* the last mission to the Moon, is launched.

1973

Tennis champ Billie Jean King defeats Bobby Riggs in the "Battle of the Sexes."

January 22 — The Supreme Court's decision in the *Roe v. Wade* case legalizes abortion.

January 27 — A cease-fire in Vietnam is announced.

May 17 — Senate hearings into Watergate open.

October 6 — Arab nations attack Israel to begin the Yom Kippur War. Arab oil producers later announce a ban on oil exports, then double prices, triggering worldwide economic crisis.

October 10 — Vice President Spiro Agnew pleads no contest to charges of tax evasion and resigns.

1974

The economy is in the worst recession in forty years.

February 4 — Patty Hearst is kidnapped.

July 24-30 — The House Judiciary Committee debates and votes for the impeachment of President Nixon.

August 9 — Nixon resigns and Vice President Gerald Ford is sworn in as president.

September 8 — Ford grants a "full, free and absolute pardon" to Richard Nixon.

1975

The United Nations declares the International Year of the Woman.

"Saturday Night Live" makes its television debut.

January 7 — North Vietnam breaks the cease-fire and attacks South Vietnam.

April 30 — South Vietnam falls to the Communists as Americans escape from Saigon in an emergency helicopter evacuation.

July 17 — U.S. and Soviet astronauts link up in a joint space mission.

1976

July 4 — Americans commemorate the two hundredth anniversary of the Declaration of Independence with a spectacular bicentennial celebration.

November 4 —Outsider Jimmy Carter narrowly defeats Gerald Ford in the presidential election.

1977

The women's movement is hit by a backlash as the ERA is defeated in several states.

The $7.7 billion trans-Alaska pipeline is opened.

Star Wars is released and becomes the most successful film of the decade.

The miniseries "Roots" draws one of the largest audiences in TV history.

January 17 — Murderer Gary Gilmore is executed, marking the first use of capital punishment in the U.S. since 1967.

August 10 — The U.S. signs the Panama Canal Treaty, agreeing to relinquish control of the canal by the end of 1999.

August 16 — Elvis Presley dies.

1978

California voters pass Proposition 13, a $7 billion cut in property taxes that sparks tax revolts in other states as well.

Muhammad Ali becomes the first man to win the world heavyweight boxing title three times.

Residents of the Love Canal community in New York State are evacuated due to dangers posed by toxic chemicals buried in the area.

September 17 — The Camp David summit between Israeli Prime Minister Begin and Egyptian President Sadat, mediated by President Carter, results in a peace accord.

November 19 — Cult leader Jim Jones and around 900 of his followers die in a mass suicide in Guyana.

1979

March 28 — A major accident at Pennsylvania's Three Mile Island nuclear power plant causes a radioactive leak.

June 18 — The U.S. and Soviet Union sign the SALT II accords limiting long-range nuclear weapons.

November 4 — Student followers of the revolutionary Muslim leader Ayatollah Khomeini seize the U.S. embassy in Iran, taking sixty-three American hostages.

December 28 — The Soviets invade Afghanistan. The SALT II arms treaty is withdrawn.

FOR FURTHER RESEARCH

Bernstein, Carl and Robert Woodward. *All the President's Men.* New York: Simon & Schuster, 1974.

Carter, Jimmy. *Keeping Faith: Memoirs of a President.* New York: Bantam Books, 1982.

Chafe, William H. *The Road to Equality: Women Since 1962 (Young Oxford History of Women in the United States, Vol 10).* New York: Oxford University Press, 1999.

Denenberg, Barry. *Voices from Vietnam.* New York: Scholastic, 1997.

Epstein, Dan. *The 70's: 20th Century Pop Culture.* Broomall, PA: Chelsea House, 2000.

Fremon, David K. *The Watergate Scandal in American History.* Springfield, NJ: Enslow, 1998.

Johnson, Charles Spurgeon. *Being and Race: Black Writing Since 1970.* Bloomington, IN: Indiana University Press, 1990.

Kelley, Robin D.G. *Into the Fire, Since 1970, Young Oxford History of African Americans.* New York: Oxford University Press, 1996.

Olson James S. (Editor), *The Historical Dictionary of the 1970s.* Westport, CT: Greenwood Publishing Group, 1999.

Sitkoff, Harvard. *PostWar America: A Student Companion.* New York: Oxford University Press, 2000.

Stewart, Gail. *The 1970s: A Cultural History of the United States.* San Diego, CA: Lucent, 1999.

Movies
The Godfather, Paramount, 1972.

Jaws, Universal Pictures/Zanuck-Brown Productions, 1975.

Taxi Driver, Columbia/Bill-Phillips/Italo-Judeo Productions, 1976.

Star Wars, LucasFilm, 1977.

Close Encounters of the Third Kind, Columbia Pictures Corp./EMI Films Ltd, 1977.

Alien, 20th Century Fox/Brandywine Productions, 1979.

Apocalypse Now, Zoetrope Studios, 1979.

Contemporary Music
Bridge Over Troubled Waters, Simon and Garfunkel, 1970.

You Are the Sunshine of My Life, Stevie Wonder, 1973.

Killing Me Softly With His Song, Roberta Flack, 1973.

Last Dance, Donna Summer, 1978.

Contemporary Literature
Bury My Heart at Wounded Knee, Dee Brown, 1971.

Fire in the Lake, Frances Fitzgerald, 1973.

Working, Studs Terkel, 1974.

Roots, Alex Haley, 1976.

The Executioner's Song, Norman Mailer, 1979.

Television
1970 *The Odd Couple*
1970 *Mary Tyler Moore Show*
1971 *All in the Family*
1972 *M*A*S*H*
1972 Munich Olympics, first televised Olympics
1973 Watergate Hearings
1974 *Happy Days*
1974 *Little House on the Prairie*
1975 *Saturday Night Live*
1977 *Roots*

Websites
The women's movement in the sixties and seventies
http://womenshistory.about.com/cs/60s70s

All about the issues of the seventies
http://www.ornl.gov/swords/seventies.html

INDEX

Page numbers in *italic* indicate picture;
page numbers in **bold** indicate
biography.

ACKNOWLEDGMENTS

The author and publishers wish to thank the following
for permission to reproduce copyright material:

Aquarius Library: 1094, 1099; The Bettmann Archive:
1078, 1096; The Bridgeman Art Library/ Frank
Stella/DACS 1995: 1103, Redferns (Mike Prior): 1092;
UPI/Bettmann Newsphotos: 1020, 1066, 1070, 1072,
1076, 1086, 1088, 1114, 1115, 1120, 1142.
All other pictures are from UPI/Bettmann.

The illustrations on pages 1037, 1039, 1057, 1134, and
1135 are by Rafi Mohammed.